Through the Year

With Saint Thérèse of Lisieux

Living the Little Way

Constant Tonnelier

Translated by Victoria Hébert
and Denis Sabourin

261
TO

Liguori

LIGUORI, MISSOURI

Published by Liguori Publications
Liguori, Missouri

Library of Congress Cataloging-in-Publication Data

Constant Tonnelier
    [Vivre l'évangile au fil des jours en disciple de sainte Thérèse de l'enfant-Jésus. English]
    Through the year with Saint Thérèse of Lisieux : living the little way / Constant Tonnelier ; translated by Victoria Hébert and Denis Sabourin. — 1st U.S. ed.
        p.   cm.
    ISBN 0-7648-0224-0
    1. Church year meditations. 2. Devotional calendars—Catholic Church. 3. Bible. N.T. Gospels—Devotional literature. I. Thérèse, de Lisieux, Saint, 1873–1897. II. Title.
BX2170.C55T6613 1998
242'.2—dc21   98–20172

This translation copyright 1998 by Liguori Publications.

First published in France as *Vivre L'Évangile au fil des jours en disciple de Sainte Thérèse de l'enfant-Jésus,* by Pierre Téqui, Paris, France.

Scriptural citations are taken from the *New Revised Standard Version Bible.* Copyright 1989 by the Division of Christian Education of the National Council of the Churches of Christ in the United States of America. Used with permission.

Printed in the United States of America
First U.S. Edition 1998
02 01 00 99 98   5 4 3 2 1

Contents

Table of Abbreviations

For *The Story of a Soul*, Autobiographical Manuscripts: Ms A, 35r (Manuscript A, folio 35, recto or front side); Ms B, 2v (Manuscript B, folio 2, verso or overleaf); Ms C, 23v (Manuscript C, folio 23, verso or overleaf).

General Correspondence: Volumes I and II: LT 28 (Thérèse's Letter No. 28).

Advice and Memories: CSG 28 (*Advice and Memories*, p. 28).

Carmel Theater: RP 3 ("Spiritual Interlude No. 3").

Poetry: PN 32 (Poem No. 32).

Prayers: Pri 12 (Prayer No. 12).

Last Conversations: DE 223 (Last Conversations, p. 223).

Last Conversations (Concordance): DE 2.8.7 (Last spoken conversation, dated August 2, seventh recorded comment).

See also, *Complete Works*, in one volume, Cerf-DDB, 1992.

Note: Long breaks in the text are marked as follows: (...). Thérèse's punctuation has been adapted for this book.

Foreword

Above all, it is the Gospel which gives me support for all of my prayers. In it, I find everything I need for my poor little soul. There, I always discover new light, hidden and mysterious knowledge (Ms A, 83v).

~

Personally, I find nothing in books except in the Gospel. That book alone is sufficient for me (DE 29) (DE 15.5.3.).

~

For a Christian, as it was for Thérèse of Lisieux, it is of great importance to use the Scriptures as a means of facing daily life. This is one of the reasons why the Church, in her liturgy, offers a text from the Scriptures as a Gospel for each day's celebration of Holy Mass. In this book we have used this model and placed texts from the daily Gospels alongside of the words of Saint Thérèse of the Child Jesus. We have selected from Saint Thérèse's works her words as they pertain to each of the daily Gospel passages. It is hoped that these two passages will add clarification and testimony to our own faith. For your further reference, a complete table of Gospel passages arranged according to the cycles of the liturgical year is listed at the back of this book with each Gospel passage listed in its usual order.

For the Sundays in Ordinary Time, we have selected Gospel references from various readings without particular reference to whether they were assigned to liturgical years A, B, or C. For the eight days preceding Christmas, the Advent O Antiphons from Scriptures have been used. For Holy Week, excerpts from the Passion of Christ as contained in the Gospel of John have been selected in order to provide continuity.

Saint Thérèse's words and thoughts are taken from her various writings, including the autobiographical manuscripts which became *The Story of a Soul*, her letters, her prayers and poetry, as well as her last conversations recorded by those who ministered to her in her last days. Each of these sources is credited at the end of the passages for daily reading.

Short prayers and reflections are also included for each day for those readers who may wish to seek further inner reflection. These prayers serve as a synthesis of the Gospel passage and words of Saint Thérèse.

The Gospel is here in these pages, in all of its life-giving strength. Saint Thérèse's spiritual doctrine is here also, an illustration, or perhaps an observation, of this power in our daily lives. Hence, the title of this book is also an explanation of its contents. It functions as a guide to living the Gospel from day to day as a follower of Saint Thérèse of the Child Jesus. By following the teachings in the Gospels in this book, the redemptive love of Jesus is revealed. It calls us to follow along Thérèse's path of love with a childlike heart. In sum, this book hopes to provide "manna" for the daily march along the pathway to the light.

About Saint Thérèse of the Child Jesus

*M*arie Françoise Thérèse Martin was born on January 2, 1873, in Alençon, in the Normandy region of France. She was the last of nine children born to Louis Martin and Zélie Guérin: a jeweler-watchmaker and a skilled lacemaker. A baby of frail health, she was baptized on Saturday, January 4, at Our Lady of Alençon Church. Only four of her siblings survived their childhood.

On August 28, 1877, her mother died and Marie became very close to her sister Pauline. Also in that same year, her family moved to Lisieux, in the Buisonnets region. In October 1882, Pauline entered into religious life there with the Carmelites.

Likewise, Marie Thérèse, in October 1886, chose the Carmelites. The holiness of Christmas that year especially affected her and it was said she was transformed; the Thérèse we all know was beginning to blossom. Her fondest wish was to enter the order, but she was only fifteen years of age. She made a personal plea to Rome, all the way to the pope, to receive special dispensation, but the outcome of that pilgrimage still left her in limbo and unsure of receiving the required permission.

On April 9, 1888, her dream became a reality and she was granted permission to enter the Carmelites in Lisieux on January 10, 1889. At that same time, her father's health was of serious concern. On Monday, September 8, 1890,

Thérèse professed her vows. She was totally devoted to the Lord: Marie Françoise Thérèse Martin became "Thérèse of the Child Jesus and of the Holy Face."

Mr. Martin died on July 29, 1894, and on September 14, Thérèse's sister Céline also entered the Carmelite order. Three of the Martin daughters were now Carmelites in Lisieux.

Thérèse had but a few years to live on this earth. She would know physical suffering and periods of barren faith, but she would also have moments of inner joy at having been called to and devoted to the love of God.

In her daily life, through the deepest humility, simplicity of heart and truth, and a daily faithfulness to her vows, she nourished her soul with the Gospels. Her choice of a religious name, "Thérèse of the Child Jesus and of the Holy Face," summed up her doctrine of spiritual childhood and her life-long fascination with the face of Christ on the cross. It was from this striking image that she came to understand God's affection for all humankind, as well as the depth of his love and forgiveness.

As a mark of obedience to her prioress, who was one of her sisters, she wrote her memoirs. Thérèse's writings, in which she shares the depth of her spiritual experience in the midst of inner struggles given through faithfulness to the love of God, have become a God-sent gift to the Church.

Around 7:20 P.M., on September 30, 1897, Thérèse left her earthly life in Lisieux, transported by love. "I am not dying, I am beginning life." She was only twenty-four years old.

Despite such a humble and short life, this Norman girl, "Thérèse of the Child Jesus and of the Holy Face," has become a Doctor of the Church and a great teacher of spiritual life.

Preface

To have the opportunity to spend the liturgical year in contemplation of the Gospel through the eyes of Saint Thérèse of Lisieux will certainly draw the many friends of this beloved saint together. Father Tonnelier has assuredly realized the dream of many of the followers of this saint through the preparation of this work.

The liturgical cycle is a wonderful reality that constantly nourishes the lifeblood which is the Church for each and every Christian. Time is not just a mindless and eternal repetition, the Incarnation of Christ has given it a meaning: His return will be the end of all time. Day by day, we are moving along, not in a repetitive and desperate universe, but towards the Promised Land—our union with the Trinitarian Lord—helped by the Word of God, our daily bread.

Thérèse of Lisieux had a keen sense of time—she loved to reflect on dates and their spiritual meaning. In her short life, Christmas, Pentecost, and the feast of the Holy Trinity were special and meaningful dates.

Therefore, it is beneficial and justified to live the liturgical cycle with Thérèse, in our quest towards the kingdom of God, already present in all of us, but whose splendor is yet to be revealed. For those who wish to delve deeper, the daily references in this book will provide a way to discover Thérèse's writings, which should prove to be an endless source of spiritual nourishment.

Many thanks to Father Tonnelier who has achieved this

exacting work with patience, care, and wisdom as an authority on Saint Thérèse. Throughout her entire life, she meditated on the Word of God and nourished her soul through it to such an extent, as Pius XI said, that she, herself, became "a Word of God for the entire world." Let us heed her words, which are an echo of the Gospel.

GUY GAUCHER
AUXILIARY BISHOP OF BAYEUX
AND LISIEUX (FRANCE)

Advent

First Sunday of Advent

"Keep awake therefore, for you do not know on what day your Lord is coming" (Mt 24:42).

～

O bright beacon of love, I know how to reach you, for I have discovered how to acquire your fire and light (Ms B, 3v).

～

Bright love of my Lord, keep me always aware so that your love makes me live each day and that on the day of your return, I will shine with your brilliant light.

First Monday of Advent

"Many will come from east and west and will eat with Abraham and Isaac and Jacob in the kingdom of heaven" (Mt 8:11).

～

Even the brightest days end in darkness, and only the first day of our final, eternal communion in heaven will be a day without a sunset (Ms A, 35v–36r).

～

Lord, allow my entire being to move forward, through both joy and sadness, so that one day I may live the full radiance of your eternal time with no end.

First Tuesday of Advent

"You have hidden these things from the wise and the intelligent and have revealed them to infants" (Lk 10:21).

～

In a moment of joy, during the days of his earthly life, Jesus exclaimed: "Father, I praise you for having hidden these things from the wise and prudent and for revealing them to the little ones." These words filled me with his great mercy. Because I was humble and weak, he came down to me and secretly instructed me in the ways of his love (Ms A, 49r).

～

You come down to the least of us to reveal your profound mystery. Lord, teach my weak and ever-changing heart about your steadfast love.

First Wednesday of Advent

"I have compassion for the crowd....I do not want to send them away hungry, for they might faint on the way" (Mt 15:32).

~

I have often noticed that Jesus doesn't come and stock me with provisions, he provides me with a new nourishment constantly, I find it within me, without even knowing how it got there....I believe simply that it is Jesus himself who is hidden in the bottom of my humble heart. He acts within me and tells me everything he wants me to do at each and every moment (Ms A, 76v).

~

Lord, in my difficult travels through daily life, may your invisible presence give me energy to move forward and make me understand the value of each and every moment.

First Thursday of Advent

"Not everyone who says to me, 'Lord, Lord,' will enter the kingdom of heaven" (Mt 7:21).

~

I understand so well that only love could make me acceptable to God, and that love is the only thing I aspire to (Ms B, 1r).

~

To voice a prayer, we use words from our human language, as you have done yourself, Jesus, but your words are seasoned by true love and reveal the depth of that love.

First Friday of Advent

"Do you believe that I am able to do this?"…"Yes, Lord"… and their eyes were opened (Mt 9:28, 30).

~

I understood that the radiance of the rose and the purity of the lily do not take away from the sweet smell of the delicate violet nor the breathtaking simplicity of the daisy (Ms A, 2v).

~

My eyes are often clouded, closed to the deepest of realities. Lord, if you do not dwell in my glance, how could I discover your beauty in all that surrounds me in so many different ways?

First Saturday of Advent

"You received without payment; give without payment" (Mt 10:8).

~

I want to be a missionary, not just for a few years, but to have been one from the creation of the world and until the end of all time....But above all, O Most Blessed Savior, I want to give my blood for you, to the very last drop (Ms B, 3r).

~

You have gone to the ultimate limits in the unselfish gift of your love, even through physical and moral suffering, and yet I sometimes complain about giving totally of myself. Lord, help me give freely of myself.

Second Sunday of Advent

This is the one of whom the prophet Isaiah spoke when he said, "The voice of one crying out in the wilderness: 'Prepare the way of the Lord, make his paths straight'" (Mt 3:3).

~

It is Jesus alone, content with my feeble efforts, who will lift me to his side. Covering me with his infinite virtue, he will make a saint of me (Ms A, 32r).

~

The road to holiness is rough and difficult. So that my efforts become a bridge to reach you, Lord, permeate them with your invigorating grace.

Second Monday of Advent

"We have seen strange things today" (Lk 5:26).

~

I have understood that Our Lord's love will reveal itself as well in the simplest soul which offers no resistance, as in the most noble (Ms A, 2v).

~

Lord, I ask that you help me look beyond the surface so that I can wonder at your marvels. Does not the ordinary become extraordinary when we learn to see it through your eyes?

Second Tuesday of Advent

"If a shepherd has a hundred sheep, and one of them has gone astray, does he not leave the ninety-nine on the mountains and go in search of the one that went astray?" (Mt 18:12).

~

My sensitive and loving heart would have easily given itself if it would have found a heart capable of understanding it (Ms A, 38r).

~

It is possible to go astray when one relies solely upon personal feelings. Happy are those who discover your uplifting mercy. Lord, help me make this discovery.

Second Wednesday of Advent

"Come to me, all you that are weary and are carrying heavy burdens, and I will give you rest" (Mt 11:28).

~

Like a mother caressing her child, in this way I will comfort you. I will carry you at my breast and caress you in my lap....Having said this, there's nothing else to say, all that's left is to weep in gratitude and love (Ms B, 1r-v).

~

Lord, at those times when I am overcome by sorrow, make me understand your comforting words. In spite of it all, make me believe in your loving presence.

Second Thursday of Advent

"The kingdom of heaven has suffered violence, and the violent take it by force" (Mt 11:12).

~

I understood that to become a saint, one must suffer a great deal, always seek perfection and forget one's self (Ms A, 10r).

~

The road to the kingdom of God is not reached through laziness, indifference, derision, or taking the easy way out. Lord, may I walk with courage.

Second Friday of Advent

"We played the flute for you, and you did not dance; we wailed, and you did not mourn" (Mt 11:17).

～

Now, nothing surprises me. I am not concerned when I see that I am weak. On the contrary, it is that weakness which glorifies me. Every day I expect to discover new imperfections within myself (Ms C, 15r).

～

Who could claim to understand such complex situations? Lord, I accept my limitations and offer them to you.

Second Saturday of Advent

"Elijah has already come, and they did not recognize him, but they did to him whatever they pleased. So also the Son of Man is about to suffer at their hands" (Mt 17:12).

～

Jesus suffered with sadness! Would a soul suffer without sadness? (...) And we would like to suffer greatly, bravely! What an illusion! (LT 89).

～

Suffering and even the possibility of suffering overwhelms me. If you were not with me, I would collapse. Lord, strengthen me!

Third Sunday of Advent

"Among those born of women no one has arisen greater than John the Baptist; yet the least in the kingdom of heaven is greater than he" (Mt 11:11).

～

God wanted to create great saints who could be compared to lilies and roses, but he also created lesser saints. They should be content to be daisies and violets, destined to simply enjoy God's glance as they lie humbly at his feet (Ms A, 2v).

～

You want me to please you, using all the abilities you have given me. For your glory and my joy, like a humble violet, I join all those who have been saved. Keep me humble, Lord.

Third Monday of Advent

"By what authority are you doing these things, and who gave you this authority?" (Mt 21:23).

~

Without seeing him or hearing his voice, Jesus teaches me in secret, not with books, because I do not understand what I read, but occasionally, I take words, such as these, from a prayer (...) which console me: "Here, I give you the Master, he will teach you all you must do. I want you to read from the book of life which contains the knowledge of love" (Ms B, 1r).

~

How could I know the right path if you don't teach me about the markers along the road? Above all, Lord, help me hear you.

Third Tuesday of Advent

"For John came to you in the way of righteousness and you did not believe him, but the tax collectors and the prostitutes believed him" (Mt 21:32).

~

I realized there were degrees of spiritual perfection and that every soul was free to respond to Our Lord's invitation by doing a little or a great deal for him; in short, to choose from the sacrifices he asks of us (Ms A, 10r-v).

~

What good is a message if it doesn't reach me? However, if I do receive what you say and respond to it, I will grow in perfection. Lord, help me understand.

Third Wednesday of Advent

"Blessed is anyone who takes no offense at me" (Lk 7:23).

~

When I make a mistake which saddens me, I know that this sadness is the result of my unfaithfulness. Do you think I stop there? Oh no, I am not that silly. I hurry to say to God: Lord, I know that I deserve this feeling of sadness, but let me offer it to you anyway as a test you have sent to me through your love. I regret my sin, but I am happy to have this suffering to offer up to you (DE 54–55) (DE 3.7.2).

~

Happy is the person who stands upright. Blessed is the sinner who does not close himself off in sadness and does not shy away from this test of Jesus' redeeming love. Lord, send me your test.

Third Thursday of Advent

"What did you go out into the wilderness to look at? A reed shaken by the wind?...Someone dressed in soft robes?... A prophet? Yes, I tell you, and more than a prophet" (Lk 7:24–26).

~

The meaning of love is to sacrifice yourself....God created children who know nothing and are only able to utter weak cries....By coming down to our level this way, God shows his infinite greatness (Ms A, 2r, 3v).

~

Our actions speak louder than our words, humble as they are. Make my whole being reflect that what I am comes from you.

Third Friday of Advent

"You sent messengers to John, and he testified to the truth.... He was a burning and shining lamp" (Jn 5:33–35).

~

Human glory is nothing. (...) I admit that I have never sought glory. My heart was attracted by self-scorn, but having recognized that, even that was too glorious; I sought oblivion (CSG 165).

~

We do not look at the light but at what it lights up. By forgetting my self and reflecting upon you, I will celebrate your glory and not my own. Lord, make me a true reflection of your will.

December 17

O Wisdom, as spoken by the Almighty, that reaches the world from end to end and arranges everything with strength and kindness, come teach us the prudent way.

~

How can a heart given to earthly affection be intimately joined to God? I think this is not possible. Not having drunk from the poisoned cup of love for earthly things, I feel that I cannot be wrong (Ms A, 38r–v).

~

Caution and wisdom teach me to use earthly things as a way to reach you. To be intimately joined with you forces me to take this effort a step further. Lord, guide my steps.

December 18

O Yahweh, Head of the House of Israel, who appeared to Moses in the flame of the burning bush and gave him the sacred laws on Sinai, come, deliver us by your powerful hand.

~

This I know: those to whom we give less, love less, but I also know that Jesus has given me more than Saint Mary Magdalene, because he gave it to me before, and this prevents me from falling (Ms A, 38v).

~

Through the flames of love, you cleanse my being and you strengthen it. By keeping me upright, Lord, instill in me your power, through love.

December 19

O Descendant of Jesse, lifted up as a standard for all peoples, before whom the kings will remain silent, and whom people will seek, come quickly to redeem us.

~

But if the son comes to know the danger from which he has been spared, will he not love him [his Father] more?

Well, I am this child, object of the provident love of a Father who did not send his Son to redeem the righteous, but the sinners (Ms A, 39r).

~

I know that I am redeemed through your love. I owe it to your provident, Fatherly love and to the glorious cross of your Son. Do not stop saving your sinful child, Lord.

December 20

O Key of David and Scepter of the House of Israel, who opens and no one closes, who closes and no one opens, come, and free the prisoner who is seated in the gloom and shadow of death.

~

The Father wants me to love him because he has given me not just a great deal, but ALL. He did not wait for me to love him like Mary Magdalene, but he wanted me to know that he had given me his inexplicable provident love so that now I am deeply in love with him (Ms A, 39r).

~

You have opened up to me the way to freedom of love. You have pulled me from the jaws of death. Lord, may your complete forgiveness bring my complete love for you.

December 21

O Light from the East, splendor of eternal light and sun of righteousness: Come, shed your light on those who are seated in the gloom and shadow of death.

∿

I heard it said that there's never been a pure soul that loved more than a repentant soul. Oh, how I would like to prove this statement wrong! (Ms A, 39r).

∿

When you shed your light into a darkened heart, the whole being is illuminated by you. Burning Sun of Love, keep me in your brightness.

December 22

O King, beloved of all nations, the cornerstone who unites the two nations, come and save the man you have made from clay.

∿

It is so easy to go astray along the flowered paths of the world...without a doubt, for an exalted soul, the gentle ness he offers is mixed with bitterness and the vast void of desire will not be filled just by momentary praise (Ms A, 40r).

~

Made out of clay contaminated with sin, I must battle not to be misled down the intriguing pathways of the world. You are my support, my cornerstone. Lord, help me fight the battles.

December 23

O Emmanuel, our King and Lawgiver, long-awaited savior of all nations, come, save us, Lord Our God.

~

I had no more hope for the "Holy Father." All the help I was finding on this earth appeared to be an arid desert, with no water. I put all my hope in God alone....I have just lived the experience that it is better to call upon Him for help than to his saints (Ms A, 66r).

~

To struggle to reach one's goals, even the best of them, to live in feverish expectation, doesn't satisfy that expectation. My only recourse, my hope, is you. Give me hope, Lord.

"Blessed be the Lord God of Israel, for he has looked favorably on his people and redeemed them" (Lk 1:68).

~

Perhaps Jesus wished to show me the world before his first visit so that I could more freely choose the way I should promise to follow him (Ms A, 32v).

~

Blessed are you for this world, to which you have come, without compromise, you have become the face of love. In freely choosing to follow you, Lord, I pray for salvation for this world.

The Octave
of Christmas
and the Epiphany

Christmas Eve

"Joseph, son of David, do not be afraid to take Mary as your wife, for the child conceived in her is from the Holy Spirit. She will bear a son, and you are to name him Jesus" (Mt 1:20–21).

～

In this brilliant night which illuminates the joy of the Holy Trinity, Jesus, the gentle little Child of the hour, will change the darkness of my soul into torrents of light (Ms A, 44v).

～

To Joseph, it was just another night. But to us, it was the Night of the ages: the Night of our lives. In coming to our world, Jesus, flood us with your light of love.

Christmas Eve Night

"To you is born this day in the city of David a Savior, who is the Messiah, the Lord" (Lk 2:11).

～

It was during this night (Christmas) when Jesus became weak and suffering for my love that he made me strong and brave. He armed me with his weapons and, since that blessed night, I have not been defeated in any battle.

To the contrary, I went from one victory to the next, to begin, more or less, "an invincible quest" (Ms A, 44v–45r).

~

Jesus, my Savior, powerful God in the guise of a fragile child, make me victorious over my weaknesses. Lead me in your "invincible quest."

Christmas Morning

But Mary treasured all these words and pondered them in her heart. The shepherds returned, glorifying and praising God for all they had heard and seen, as it had been told them (Lk 2:19–20).

~

During this Christmas night (…) Jesus accomplished, in one instant, the work that I could not do in ten years. Jesus did it relying upon my good faith, which has never failed me (Ms A, 45v).

~

Like those who take credit for nothing, but who pray, glorify and praise you, I give you my good faith, Jesus, by letting you mold me. Accept my faith.

Christmas Day

And the Word became flesh and lived among us, and we have seen his glory (Jn 1:14).

~

Oh Divine Word, you are the beloved Eagle that I adore and am drawn to! You have come down to this world of exile to suffer and die in order to lead all souls to the eternal home of the Blessed Trinity (Ms B, 5v).

~

Light of Splendor, Word of Resounding Echoes, Divine Word, beloved Eagle, lead me to praise the Holy Trinity in the depths of my soul.

December 26

"And you will be hated by all because of my name. But the one who endures to the end will be saved" (Mt 10:22).

~

I understand that true greatness is found in one's soul and not in one's name. (…) Thus, it is in heaven that we will find our true value. Then, "each of us will receive our just reward from God." He who has chosen to be the poorest

*and most forgotten for the sake of Jesus on earth, will
become the first, the noblest, and the richest (Ms A, 56r).*

~

My worthiness is etched in the poverty and anonymity of
my life at your service. You will reveal my true value to me
on the final judgment day, if I remain steadfast to the end.
Lord, support me, help me to remain true.

December 27

Then the other disciple, who reached the tomb first, also
went in, and he saw and believed (Jn 20:8).

~

*Today, as I enjoy the solitude of Carmel (resting in the
shadow of He whom I so ardently desire), I find that I
have bought my happiness at a small price. I would be
ready to go through the hardest of trials to acquire this,
if I did not already have it (Ms A, 53v).*

~

Jesus, you are the inner happiness of a heart which loves,
the guiding light of one who believes. You inspire silence
and solitude in one who sees the invisible. You are all of
that for me every day.

December 28

Herod sent and killed all the children in and around Bethle-hem who were two years old or under, according to the time that he had learned from the wise men (Mt 2:16).

∽

Like baby birds learn to sing by listening to their parents, similarly, children learn virtue, the subtle song of divine love, from those souls who have been given the task to shape their lives (Ms A, 53r).

∽

If the Holy Innocents glorified God in song through their death, I proclaim your love in a symphony with my brothers and sisters. Lord, teach me the song you want me to sing.

December 29

"For my eyes have seen your salvation, which you have pre-pared in the presence of all peoples" (Lk 2:30–31).

∽

The story of my soul: To begin to tell what will be my task for all eternity: to recount the story of God's mercies (Ms A, 2r).

∽

Christ, the salvation that you give me will be to stand at your side and give eternal thanks, to proclaim your mercies and all-encompassing love. Lord, let me voice your mercies to the world.

December 30

Anna...never left the temple but worshiped there with fasting and prayer night and day (Lk 2:36–37).

~

How wonderful is the vocation whose goal is to preserve knowledge destined just for souls! This is the vocation of the Carmelites. The singular goal of our prayers and sacrifices is to be the apostles of the apostles, praying for them as they convert souls by their words and, above all, by their deeds (Ms A, 56r–v).

~

Each of us can contribute to the apostolate of the Church through prayer. Some may pray in inner silence in their daily life and some in the solitude of a cloister. Lord, help me accomplish my vocation faithfully.

December 31

In him was life, and the life was the light of all people. The light shines in the darkness, and the darkness did not overcome it (Jn 1:4–5).

~

Divine Word, you have ascended to that inaccessible light which is your dwelling place from this day onward. You also remain with us in this valley of tears, hidden under the appearance of the sacred host....Eternal Eagle, you want to nourish me with your divine sustenance— me, that poor little being, who would be nothing without your Divine glance which gives me life (Ms B, 5v).

~

Oh Word of Life, take me to where you dwell by nourishing me with your body and your blood. Eternal Eagle, take me into the aura of your loving glance.

Holy Family Sunday

The child grew and became strong, filled with wisdom; and the favor of God was upon him (Lk 2:40).

~

The path of spiritual childhood is a road of trust and surrender. I wish to teach [the souls] about the small ways that have worked for me. I want to tell them there is just one thing to do here below on earth: to shower Jesus with the flowers of their small sacrifices, to win him over with small tokens of affection (DE 223) (DE 17.7.2).

~

It is on the path of spiritual childhood that I learn to trust in the Lord and surrender my whole being to him. Lord, mold me as you wish.

January 1

After eight days had passed, it was time to circumcise the child; and he was called Jesus, the name given by the angel before he was conceived in the womb (Lk 2:21).

~

For some time now, I had offered myself to the Child Jesus as his little toy. I had asked him not to use me as a prized toy, one that children are usually satisfied just to look at without touching, but as a small ball of little value that he can throw down to the ground, kick, puncture, leave in a corner or press to his heart, if it should please him (Ms A, 64r).

~

My name identifies me but, moreover, I am what your heart chooses me to be. Lord, use me as you will. Throughout this year, may I bring you joy.

January 2

"I baptize with water. Among you stands one whom you do not know, the one who is coming after me; I am not worthy to untie the thong of his sandal" (Jn 1:26–27).

~

My heart aspired to other marvels. I had sufficiently contemplated the beauties of the earth. Now I seek the beauty of heaven. I was ready to become a prisoner in order to give this heavenly beauty to other souls (Ms A, 67r).

~

While my path is filled with wonders, I aim to discover you. You are hidden. Heavenly Beauty, guide my search.

January 3

The next day he saw Jesus coming toward him and declared, "Here is the Lamb of God who takes away the sin of the world!" (Jn 1:29).

~

Jesus, if it is so delightful to want to love you, what it must be like to possess and enjoy Divine Love!...How can an imperfect soul such as mine hope to have the fulfillment of Divine Love?...O Jesus, my first and only friend, my ONLY love, explain this mystery to me (Ms B, 4v).

~

By taking away the sins of the world, removing me from all sin, you invite me to love you. My ever-present friend, open my heart to your love.

January 4

"Rabbi" (which translated means Teacher), "where are you staying?"..."Come and see." They came and saw where he was staying, and they remained with him that day. It was about four o'clock in the afternoon (Jn 1:38–39).

~

Now, I have no other desire than to love Jesus deeply. (...) I do not wish to suffer or die, however I love both of these, but it is love that attracts me....I have desired these for a long time. (...) Now, I am guided by surrender alone, I have no other point of reference! (Ms A, 82v–83r).

~

How can I discover you if you don't guide me to you and I don't surrender totally? Lord, when we meet in prayer, join my will to yours.

January 5

Philip found Nathanael and said to him, "We have found him about whom Moses in the law and also the prophets wrote, Jesus son of Joseph from Nazareth" (Jn 1:45).

~

So that is all that Jesus wants from us, he does not need our accomplishments, only our love. (…) He thirsts for love (Ms B, 1v).

~

The main task you ask of me is to reveal to my brothers and sisters that you are Divine Love and that you want their love. Bless my task.

January 6

Jesus was about thirty years old when he began his work. He was the son (as was thought) of Joseph…son of Adam, son of God (Lk 3:23–38).

~

Above all, it is the Gospel which gives me support for all of my prayers. Through the Word, all the needs of my poor soul are met. In mysterious and hidden ways, I always discover new light and life (Ms A , 83v).

~

Jesus, you are not just what you appear to be. The Gospel helps us uncover the mystery of you. I must delve deeper. May the Gospel sustain my prayers every day.

January 7

"They have no wine."…"Woman, what concern is that to you and to me? My hour has not yet come."…"Do whatever he tells you" (Jn 2:3–5).

∼

Yes, all is well when we seek only the will of Jesus (Ms C, 2v).

∼

O Jesus, did your mother, Mary, force your hand? Has the time come for you to do your Father's will? You declare it at Cana and call upon us to do what your heart says. Lord, help us hear your call.

Epiphany of the Lord

When they had heard the king, they set out; and there, ahead of them, went the star that they had seen at its rising, until it stopped over the place where the child was. When they saw that the star had stopped, they were overwhelmed with joy. On entering the house, they saw the child with Mary his mother; and they knelt down and paid him homage. Then, opening their treasure chests, they offered him gifts of gold, frankincense, and myrrh (Mt 2:9–11).

~

Oh Jesus, my Beloved! How tender and sweet you are in the treatment of my humble soul! How pleased you are to make your grace shine even in the midst of the darkest storm (Ms B, 2r).

~

I am guided by the star, like the three Wise Men. On my sometimes dark road, a beam of grace follows me to help discover you. Make me find your light.

Monday After the Epiphany

"The people who sat in darkness have seen a great light, and for those who sat in the region and shadow of death light has dawned" (Mt 4:16).

~

As a child of light, I have understood that my wish to be everything at once, to embrace all vocations, is a type of wealth which could tend to make me unfair to others. So, I have decided to use this wealth to make friends in the Lord (Ms B, 4r).

~

Under scrutiny, things appear in a different light. Lord, may I help others discover who they are in your eyes, by sharing the light you have given to me.

Tuesday After the Epiphany

Taking the five loaves and the two fish, he looked up to heaven, and blessed and broke the loaves, and gave them to his disciples to set before the people; and he divided the two fish among them....All ate and were filled (Mk 6:41–42).

~

The time of my first Communion is etched deeply in my heart. I could not have been in a better state of mind.... Jesus wanted me to experience as perfect a joy as possible in this earthly valley of tears (Ms A, 32v).

~

Lord, to me, you will always be the God that gives signs. However, through the Eucharist, you are truly here. Make me hunger for you. Let me taste the joy of your presence.

After saying farewell to them, he went up on the mountain to pray (Mk 6:46).

~

When dark clouds come to hide the Star of Love, the small bird doesn't move because he knows that the Sun still shines behind those clouds and that its true brightness will not be overshadowed for one single moment (Ms B, 5r).

~

The hardships of life may close my heart to you, just as the mountain hides the sun, but I know that nothing can ever block your presence. Here and now, Lord, I pray to you.

Then Jesus, filled with the power of the Spirit, returned to Galilee, and a report about him spread through all the surrounding country. He began to teach in their synagogues and was praised by everyone (Lk 4:14–15).

~

Oh Jesus, leave me in the excess of my gratitude, let me praise the depth of your love….Seeing such depth of love, how could my heart not leap out to you? How could my trust have limits? (Ms B, 5v).

~

As I pass through my life with you, how could I not speak of all the blessings you have given me? I trust completely in you. My heart constantly renews its love for you. Lord, thank you.

But now more than ever the word about Jesus spread abroad; many crowds would gather to hear him and to be cured of their diseases. But he would withdraw to deserted places and pray (Lk 5:15–16).

~

Jesus is happy to show me the only road to this Divine warmth. This path is one of complete surrender, like a child who sleeps without fear in his Father's arms (Ms B, 1r).

~

All-Powerful Lord, the path to you is one of prayer and surrender to your holy will. As the child confidently sleeps in his father's arms, listening to his soothing words, I entrust you with my life.

"He who has the bride is the bridegroom. The friend of the bridegroom, who stands and hears him, rejoices greatly at the bridegroom's voice. For this reason my joy has been fulfilled" (Jn 3:29).

~

Oh Jesus, to be your bride, to be a Carmelite, to become the mother of all souls through my union with you, should satisfy me...however, such is not the case.... Without a doubt, these three privileges are my vocation. Yet, within me, I feel the need for other vocations (Ms B, 2v).

~

Jesus, to be connected to you with such strong, loving bonds as I have in the community of life, opens my horizons to the work you call me to do along with those others called to do the same through your love. Strengthen my connection to you.

The Baptism of the Lord

When Jesus had been baptized...suddenly the heavens were opened to him and he saw the Spirit of God descending like a dove and alighting on him. And a voice from heaven said, "This is my Son, the Beloved, with whom I am well pleased" (Mt 3:16–17).

~

The knowledge of love, oh yes, these words echo softly in the ear of my soul. I do not want to think of anything but this knowledge. Having given all my wealth to this, like the bride of the blessed canticles, I feel I have given nothing at all (Ms B, 1r).

~

Father, you put all of your love in your Son who saw the cross as a sign of loving obedience. The Spirit of Love is the bond between the Father and the Son. Holy Trinity, teach me the knowledge of Divine Love.

Lent

Ash Wednesday

"But whenever you pray, go into your room and shut the door and pray to your Father who is in secret; and your Father who sees in secret will reward you" (Mt 6:6).

～

Gratitude is the one thing which disposes God to grant his blessings. If we thank him for his graces, he is grateful and showers us with ten more. If we continue in this manner, with the same enthusiasm, imagine the incalculable multitude of blessings! I have done this. Try it and you will see. My gratitude is limitless for all he has given me and I show it to him in a thousand ways (CSG 72).

～

You show me the multitude of your blessings when I am alone with you. Is this your way to prompt me to be more generous in my service to you? Lord, let me serve you.

Thursday After Ash Wednesday

"For those who want to save their life will lose it, and those who lose their life for my sake will save it" (Lk 9:24).

～

There are certain souls who require regular payment. For me, I take my chances at the bank of Love....I go for the big

*win. If I lose, I will know. I don't concern myself with the ups
and downs, Jesus takes care of them for me. I do not know
if I am rich or poor but I will know this later (CSG 71).*

⌣

This give and take is not an expression of love. I must completely empty myself and lose my sense of self, to love you
in the way you love me. I must become a pauper in antici-
pation of the wealth a life of love will give me. Lord, help
me love you as you love me.

Friday After Ash Wednesday

"The days will come when the bridegroom is taken away
from them, and then they will fast" (Mt 9:15).

⌣

*We have heard loving complaints from your beloved
mouth. Understanding that the thirst which consumes
you is one of love, we want to quench it and possess an
infinite love! Blessed Husband of our souls! If we had
the love from all the hearts, all that love would be for
you....Give us this love and quench your thirst through
your humble brides (Pri 12).*

⌣

Blessed Soul-Spouse, I have fasted in mourning for your
absence. Break my fast, quench my thirst with your eternal love.

Saturday After Ash Wednesday

"I have come to call not the righteous but sinners to repentance" (Lk 5:32).

~

When you are angry with someone, the way to find peace is to pray for that person and ask God to reward them for making you suffer. In spite of all their efforts to better themselves, God leaves certain souls with weaknesses because it would be detrimental if they had virtues others could see in them (CSG 150).

~

You came for sinners. I am a sinner who is easily angered by others. I don't know how to find peace through prayer. I don't easily accept my weaknesses. Lord, give me peace.

First Sunday of Lent

Then Jesus was led up by the Spirit into the wilderness to be tempted by the devil (Mt 4:1).

~

The more you press forward, the less you have to fight, or rather, the easier you win because you see the good side of things. It is then that your soul rises above the humans. It is incredible how, in the end, everything anyone tells

me doesn't even graze my soul because I have under-
stood the weakness of human judgment (CSG 186).

~

I am afraid to venture into spiritual battles. The Tempter acts in subtle ways and turns things all around. Triumphant Jesus, take care of the problems which block my way so I can go forward with you.

First Monday of Lent

"Lord, when was it that we saw you….and did not take care of you?"…"Truly I tell you, just as you did not do it to one of the least of these…" (Mt 25:44–45).

~

See those ugly pears, they are the image of the Sisters you dislike. When we rid them of their imperfections and give them to you, you are happy to eat them. On judgment day, in the same way, you will be amazed to see your Sisters who have had their imperfections removed. In your eyes, you will see them as great saints (CSG 108).

~

On judgment day, in the Divine Light of God, I will be astonished and in awe of you, Lord. If I can put love into all I do for you, then I will be doing your Holy Will. If not, all will be for nothing. Lord, help me put love into all I do.

First Tuesday of Lent

"Pray then in this way: Our Father in heaven....Your kingdom come" (Mt 6:9–10).

~

Oh, happy carefree ecstacy of love! Love gives all and trusts! But often, we don't give spontaneously, we hesitate to sacrifice our temporal and spiritual comforts. This isn't really love! Love is blind; it is a torrent that eliminates everything in its path (CSG 62).

~

As a child of the Heavenly Father, am I ready to sacrifice my own interests for God's, so that his kingdom will come? The Father waits for my honest and generous love. Let me give it freely and without concern.

First Wednesday of Lent

"The people of Nineveh...repented at the proclamation of Jonah, and see, something greater than Jonah is here!" (Lk 11:32).

~

You will not succeed in practicing virtue: You want to climb a mountain while God wants to send you to the bottom of a fertile valley where you will learn about self-contempt (CSG 26).

~

To repent does not mean to commit to a lifelong heroic program. It is simply letting God's blessing of love into your heart. Lord, open my heart to your blessings.

First Thursday of Lent

"If you then, who are evil, know how to give good gifts to your children, how much more will your Father in heaven give good things to those who ask him!" (Mt 7:11).

~

In our childhood, we must learn to recognize what God wants from our souls. We must support the action of his blessings, without ever slowing it down or getting ahead of it (CSG 7).

~

As a child relies upon his family for his upbringing, I rely upon you, Lord, to teach me about life. Without anticipating your action or causing you to slow down, I ask your kind blessings.

First Friday of Lent

"So when you are offering your gift at the altar, if you remember that your brother or sister has something against you, leave your gift there before the altar and go; first be reconciled to your brother or sister, and then come and offer your gift" (Mt 5:23–24).

∽

If you always want to be right, you do this to the detriment of your soul. And to tell others what to do, even if you are truly right, still puts you in conflict. Yours is not to control other people's behavior. You must not set yourself up as a judge—that is God's right alone—your only mission is to be an angel of peace (CSG 106).

∽

If I set myself up as judge, all dialogue will end. The path of kindness is reopened by reconciliation and healing. Lord, let me be that messenger of peace.

First Saturday of Lent

"If you love those who love you, what reward do you have? Do not even the tax collectors do the same? And if you greet only your brothers and sisters, what more are you doing than others?" (Mt 5:46–47).

∽

You say you want to be good with those who are good, gentle with those who are gentle. And when someone disagrees with you, you strike out against them....On the contrary: "Do good for those who hate you, pray for those who persecute you" (CSG 103).

~

A sign of God's presence is the ability to be even tempered with all, kind to the bothersome, and truly charitable with those different from ourselves. Lord, grant me this ability.

Second Sunday of Lent

Later, Jesus took with him Peter and James and his brother John and led them up a high mountain, by themselves. And he was transfigured before them, and his face shone like the sun, and his clothes became dazzling white (Mt 17:1–2).

~

Oh Holy Face, more beautiful than the lilies and spring roses! You are not hidden from us! The tears which come from your Divine Face are like diamonds...of infinite value. We want to gather them so we can buy back the souls of our brothers and sisters (Pri 12).

~

Transfigured Face of Jesus, draw me to you. Disfigured Face of the Passion, lead me into the painful redemption.

Second Monday of Lent

"Give, and it will be given to you. A good measure, pressed down, shaken together, running over, will be put into your lap; for the measure you give will be the measure you get back" (Lk 6:38).

～

You must do all that is in you, give without measure, constantly sacrifice, to prove one's love by all the good deeds in one's power. It is necessary, when we have done all that we believe we must do, to think of ourselves as "useless servants," all the while hoping that God will give us, by his grace, all that we desire. This is what the little souls hope to do, as they "run" along the path of spiritual childhood (CSG 50).

～

To give something to another is good. To give of oneself, without measure, is the true yardstick of love. This is the path of spiritual childhood. Lord, show me this path.

Second Tuesday of Lent

"You are all students….Nor are you to be called instructors, for you have one instructor, the Messiah" (Mt 23:8–10).

～

I must seek out the company of certain Sisters who are most disagreeable to me. (…) A word or a friendly smile, often that's all it takes to soothe a sad soul. But, I don't practice kindness just to reach this goal. (…) Even the nicest of words may be misinterpreted. To please Jesus (…) I want to be friendly with everyone (Ms C, 28r–v).

〜

One reality unites us all and goes beyond the words we use in our lives: We are all brothers and sisters. May my kindness toward others testify to my charity in Jesus.

Second Wednesday of Lent

"You will indeed drink my cup, but to sit at my right hand and at my left, this is not mine to grant, but it is for those for whom it has been prepared by my Father" (Mt 20:23).

〜

Since it had been necessary for Christ to suffer so that he would enter through that into glory, you must also drink from his same chalice if you want to have a place at his side (Ms A, 62v).

〜

To drink at the cup of the moral suffering of the Passion means that one must reject sin and enter into Christ's battle against evil. Lord, Let me fight that battle at your side.

Second Thursday of Lent

"Father Abraham, have mercy on me, and send Lazarus to dip the tip of his finger in water and cool my tongue; for I am in agony in these flames" (Lk 16:24).

~

I knew this could not glorify him [to be cast into hell] since he only wants our happiness. But when we love, we feel the need to speak a thousand foolish words. If I spoke that way, it was not that I did not seek heaven, but then, my heaven is nothing other than love (Ms A, 52v).

~

We are created for Eternal Love. Those who deny Love will have terrible suffering on judgment day. Lord, have mercy on those still to be saved by your forgiveness.

Second Friday of Lent

"Therefore I tell you, the kingdom of God will be taken away from you and given to a people that produces the fruits of the kingdom" (Mt 21:43).

~

We must plant seeds of goodness around us, without concern for what may grow from them. It is up to us to work, and for Jesus to enjoy the success. Do not fear battle when it will bring good to your neighbors. Resume it anyhow, in spite of the desire for personal peace. Do not do it just to open the eyes of the novices, but above all, do it to serve God (CSG 8).

∽

Above all, I must not remain inactive in my service for the kingdom of God just because my conviction seeks stimulation and my personal peace will suffer. Lord, you expect each of us to do our part.

Second Saturday of Lent

"Father, I have sinned against heaven and before you; I am no longer worthy to be called your son; treat me like one of your hired hands" (Lk 15:18–19).

∽

The father [who is a skilled doctor], knowing that there is a stone on the road in front of his son, hurries there to remove it without being seen by anyone. Certainly this son, the object of his father's farsighted tenderness, not knowing the peril from which his father spared him, will not be able to show him his gratitude. Thus, his love for his father may not grow as much as if he had been healed by him directly (Ms A, 38v–39r).

∽

Father, you are so subtle that I may not be able to see all the farsighted tenderness you give me along my way. Nevertheless, my love for you grows. Lord, help me to see your tenderness.

Third Sunday of Lent

"If you knew the gift of God, and who it is that is saying to you, 'Give me a drink,' you would have asked him, and he would have given you living water" (Jn 4:10).

~

Jesus only needs our love, not our deeds. That same God who claims he does not need to let us know when he is hungry, was not afraid to beg the Good Samaritan for a drink of water. He was thirsty....When he said: "Give me a drink," the Creator of the universe was asking his humble creature for her love. He was thirsty for love (Ms B, 1v).

~

Jesus, if I only knew how you thirst for my love. If I only understood that your heart is a prolific spring of living water. Lord, I know that love calls for love and yet I still greedily measure the portions I give you. I pray that you open my heart.

And he said, "Truly I tell you, no prophet is accepted in the prophet's hometown" (Lk 4:24).

~

Oh, I feel it, Jesus is even thirstier than ever! He only encounters thankless and indifferent people among his followers and disciples. Alas, among his disciples, he finds few hearts given to him without reservation and who understand the tenderness of his infinite Love (Ms B, 1v).

~

It is disappointing to be misunderstood by your neighbors. It is even more painful to be misunderstood by your loved ones. God of tenderness, make me grasp the depth of your love, show me how to welcome it. Help me to understand you more fully.

Third Tuesday of Lent

"Then his lord summoned him and said to him, 'You wicked slave! I forgave you all that debt because you pleaded with me. Should you not have had mercy on your fellow slave, as I had mercy on you?'" (Mt 18:32–33).

~

I prefer to be unjustly accused when I have done nothing wrong, and offer this up to God with joy. Afterwards, I am shocked at the thought that I was capable of doing the very thing I was accused of doing (CSG 19).

~

Only God can forgive time and time again. I have been forgiven by you, Lord, numerous times. Without this, I would surely be unable to show mercy for others. This humbles me. Help me to remain humble.

Third Wednesday of Lent

"Whoever does [the commandments] and teaches them will be called great in the kingdom of heaven" (Mt 5:19).

~

Jesus is my guiding force. (…) He teaches me to do everything through love, to refuse him nothing, and to be happy when he gives me the chance to prove my love for him. However, this is done in peace, without consideration. Jesus does it all, I do nothing (LT 142).

~

Nothing is too small when it is done out of love because each gesture is a proof of love. I must take advantage of all opportunities to do little kindnesses so they become true acts of love in my heart. Lord, help me give my all to you without a second thought.

Third Thursday of Lent

"Whoever is not with me is against me, and whoever does not gather with me scatters" (Lk 11:23).

~

If we are having problems with a disagreeable soul, don't get disheartened or abandon it. We must always keep our wit sharp so we can lead that poor soul to the right path. Don't quit fighting even when you have little hope of winning. Success is not important. God asks us to fight to the very end, to overlook our fatigue, and not let up or be discouraged (DE 21) (DE 6.4.2).

~

Brotherly love cares about what others do. How can I accept that someone is wasting their life? Lord, give me the strength to fight for you, using the sharpness of my wit.

Third Friday of Lent

"Hear, O Israel: the Lord our God, the Lord is one; you shall love the Lord your God....You shall love your neighbor as yourself. There is no other commandment greater than these" (Mk 12:29–31).

~

I know no other path to perfection than love....Our heart is made for love! (…) There is only One who could understand the depth of the word love!...Only Jesus knows how to give us infinitely more than we give him (LT 109).

~

Dear Lord, you are love. You make us drink at your wellspring of love so we can live through you and love each other. Love is everything in our lives. You made us to love. Lord, quench us at your well of love.

Third Saturday of Lent

"The Pharisee, standing by himself, was praying. (…) The tax collector was standing far off....'God, be merciful to me, a sinner!'...Those who exalt themselves will be humbled, but all who humble themselves will be exalted" (Lk 18:11, 13–14).

~

It seems to me that humility is truth. I don't know if I am truly humble, but I feel that I see the truth in all things (CSG 19).

~

Certainly a path to humility is to be true to oneself and to recognize one's limitations and sins. Lord, let me lean on you as I walk the path to humility. Help me to grow.

Fourth Sunday of Lent

"Do you believe in the Son of Man?"..."And who is he, sir? Tell me, so that I may believe in him."..."You have seen him, and the one speaking with you is he."..."Lord, I believe" (Jn 9:35–38).

~

Wasn't Jesus my only real friend? I knew only how to speak to him. Conversations with humans, even devout conversations, tired my soul....I felt that talking to God was better than talking about God because we humans put so much self-importance into these spiritual conversations (Ms A, 40v–41r).

~

My life of faith is built by discovering you, not just by speaking about you, Lord. Because I believe in you, Jesus, speaking to you will give me confidence. Let us speak every day.

Fourth Monday of Lent

The official said to him, "Sir, come down before my little boy dies." Jesus said to him, "Go; your son will live." The man believed the word that Jesus spoke to him and started on his way (Jn 4:49–50).

~

The only way to our happiness and proof of our love is to keep the word of Jesus. But what is his word? It seems to me that Jesus is the Word, himself....Jesus, himself, the Word, the Word of God! (...) From this we know what Word we must follow. (...) We must keep Jesus in our hearts (LT 165).

~

To have faith in someone's word, we must first have faith in the person who speaks it. To keep your word in my heart is to keep your presence in me, Lord. Jesus, Son of God, who lives within me, strengthen my faith in you.

Fourth Tuesday of Lent

"See, you have been made well! Do not sin any more, so that nothing worse happens to you" (Jn 5:14).

~

On leaving the confessional, I felt so content and so light. I had never before felt such joy in my soul. Since then, I have returned to confession on all the great feast days. It was a real feast for me each time I went (Ms A, 17r).

~

Is there anything more valuable than good health? Blessed are you, Lord of mercy, for the spiritual health the Church gives us in your name through the sacrament of reconciliation. Make me live it in joy and celebration so that it will open my soul for my future through you.

Fourth Wednesday of Lent

"I tell you, anyone who hears my word and believes him who sent me has eternal life, and does not come under judgment, but has passed from death to life" (Jn 5:24).

~

Yes, I see it clearly....It's the image of love God has for me. I have never given him anything but love, so he gives me love. It doesn't finish there, he will soon give me even more. This touches me deeply. It's like a ray, or rather a bolt of lightning in the midst of my gloom....But only like a flash (DE 88) (DE 22.7.1).

~

Your word, Lord, is love. When I listen to it, it is like a flash, lighting my way just long enough for me to know you are there. Let this current of love pass from me to others.

Fourth Thursday of Lent

"I do not accept glory from human beings. How can you believe when you accept glory from one another and do not seek the glory that comes from the one who alone is God?" (Jn 5:41, 44).

~

God helped me feel that the only real glory is the one which lasts forever. To achieve that, it is not necessary to perform any great exploits but to live a quiet life and practice your faith in such a way that your left hand doesn't know what your right hand does (Ms A, 32r).

~

Where is my glory? Is it in a display of wealth, or in praise I have received? No. True glory is built on humble day-to-day activities, hidden from others. This will only be revealed when I appear before your glory. Lord, make me a humble instrument of your true glory.

Fourth Friday of Lent

"You know me, and you know where I am from. I have not come on my own. But the one who sent me is true, and you do not know him. I know him, because I am from him, and he sent me" (Jn 7:28–29).

~

I have never acted as Pilate did when he refused to hear the truth. I have always said to God, "My Lord, I want to hear you well, I beg of you, answer me when I humbly ask: what is the truth?" Make me see things as they really are. Let nothing cloud my sight (DE 88) (DE 21.7.4).

~

We hide the truth from ourselves or it may be hidden from us by others. But, we can only build our lives on truth. Lord, help me see the truth in all things.

Fourth Saturday of Lent

When they heard these words, some in the crowd said, "This is really the prophet. Never has anyone spoken like this!" (Jn 7:40, 46).

~

I know from experience, "That the kingdom of God is inside us." Jesus, (…) the Doctor of all doctors, teaches without words….I have never heard him speak but I know he is inside me. At each and every moment, he guides me to do what I must do. Just when I need it, I discover lights I had never seen before (Ms A, 83v).

~

Word of God, by your silent presence, you reveal the mystery of the Holy Trinity to me. Make my heart understand.

Fifth Sunday of Lent

"I am the resurrection and the life. Those who believe in me, even though they die, will live, and everyone who lives and believes in me will never die" (Jn 11:25–26).

～

Adored Face, since you are the only home for our souls, our hymns will not be sung on foreign soil. While we await eternity when we will gaze upon your infinite glory, our only desire is to enchant your Divine Eyes while hiding our faces so no one can recognize us....Your veiled glance, that is our heaven, Oh Jesus! (Pri 12).

～

Jesus, veiled glance of faith, help me travel life's rough roads with the assurance that I will see your face in eternity. You are my song of hope. Let me find my resurrection in you.

Fifth Monday of Lent

"Has no one condemned you?"..."No one, sir."..."Neither do I condemn you. Go your way, and from now on do not sin again" (Jn 8:10–11).

～

Oh Lord, Blessed Trinity, I want to love you and make you loved, to work toward the glorification of the Holy

Church by saving souls on earth and by delivering those who suffer in purgatory. I want to fulfill your will perfectly. (…) I would like to be a saint, but I feel my powerlessness. I ask you, my Lord, to be my saintliness (Pri 6).

~

You don't condemn sinners. Instead, you save them by offering a future in you. Help me do your will by uniting me to the mission of redemption of your Beloved Son.

Fifth Tuesday of Lent

"You will die in your sins unless you believe that I am he. When you have lifted up the Son of Man, then you will realize that I am he" (Jn 8:24, 28).

~

Because you have loved me to the point of giving your only Son to me as my Savior and Spouse, the infinite treasure of his graces are also mine. I gladly offer these to you, begging that you look at me only through the Holy Face of Jesus and in his burning heart of love (Pri 6).

~

Father, the cross carries the bruised body of Jesus. His bloody face shows his suffering. Grant me salvation through the merit of his Easter as your only Son. Draw me to the heights of your Divine Love.

Fifth Wednesday of Lent

"The slave does not have a permanent place in the household; the son has a place there forever. So if the Son makes you free, you will be free indeed" (Jn 8:35–36).

~

Oh Blessed Trinity, I offer you love and the merits of the Blessed Virgin. I send my offering to her, and ask her to present it to you. During the days of his earthly life, her Divine Son, my Blessed Spouse, told us, "All that you ask of my Father in my name, he will give you." Thus, I am certain that you will grant my desires (Pri 6).

~

Through the Son, we have become children of God, now and forever, in the house of the living God. Through the communion of the Blessed Son, the source of all gifts, we have become both children as well as brothers and sisters. I freely offer you my life, as a humble petition, through the intercession of the Blessed Virgin.

Fifth Thursday of Lent

"Very truly, I tell you, whoever keeps my word will never see death" (Jn 8:51).

~

In my heart, I feel great desire. With all confidence, I ask you to come take possession of my soul. I can't receive Holy Communion as often as I would like, but Lord, aren't you all-powerful? Remain with me, as you do at the tabernacle. Do not ever leave your little Host (Pri 6).

~

Lord, the call I receive when I faithfully listen to your word is to live inthe intense desire to be eternally united with you. Lord, let me live in and for you.

Fifth Friday of Lent

"I have shown you many good works from the Father. For which of these are you going to stone me?" (Jn 10:32).

~

I want to console you for the ingratitude of wicked people. I beg you to take away from me the freedom to displease you. If I occasionally stumble out of weakness, I ask that you quickly purify my soul by your divine glance, removing all my imperfections, like a fire that consumes everything within its flames (Pri 6).

~

When I don't recognize the many graces you have given me along the path of life, I break your heart, God of love. Help me to hear your cries. Renew me through your love.

Fifth Saturday of Lent

"It is better for you to have one man die for the people than to have the whole nation destroyed" (Jn 11:50).

~

My Lord, I thank you for all the blessings you have granted me, in particular, for having me pass the stringent test of suffering. On judgment day, I will think of you carrying the scepter of the cross. As you have judged me worthy to share this most precious cross with you, when I am in heaven, I hope to look like you and see my body glorified with the blessed wounds of your Passion (Pri 6).

~

God-made-man, the cross stands as both a symbol of your suffering as well as one of victory. By leaning on your cross, I will be able to carry my own crosses in the hope of sharing your glory in renewed life. Lord, let me lean on you.

Palm Sunday

Then they brought the colt to Jesus and threw their cloaks on it; and he sat on it....Then those who went ahead and those who followed were shouting, "Hosanna! Blessed is the one who comes in the name of the Lord! Blessed is the coming kingdom of our ancestor David! Hosanna in the highest heaven!" (Mk 11:7, 9–10).

~

After being exiled on earth, I hope to go and rejoice in your presence in our Father's house. However, I do not want to gain merits just for heaven. I want to work for your Divine Love for the sole purpose of pleasing you, consoling your Sacred Heart and saving souls who will love you for all eternity (Pri 6).

~

You are my Savior. I follow your path. All of my "hosannas" repeat my love to you. Let me unite myself with you for the good of all humankind. Make it possible for me to live with you in the kingdom to come.

Monday of Holy Week

Mary took a pound of costly perfume made of pure nard, anointed Jesus' feet, and wiped them with her hair. The house was filled with the fragrance of the perfume (Jn 12:3).

~

Lord, at the twilight of this life, I will appear to you with empty hands because I do not ask you to keep count of my good deeds. All of our laws are flawed in your eyes. I would like, then, to cloak myself with your law and from your love, receive you for eternity. I want no other crown than you (Pri 6).

~

At the end of my life, you will find nothing in my hands but the perfume of my love. Lord, judge me worthy enough to delight in your love forever.

Tuesday of Holy Week

"Now the Son of Man has been glorified, and God has been glorified in him. If God has been glorified in him, God will also glorify him in himself" (Jn 13:31–32).

~

To you, time has no meaning. A single day is like a thousand years. In a single moment, you could prepare me to appear before you....In order to live within an act of perfect love, I offer myself in sacrifice to your merciful love, begging you to consume me endlessly, letting my soul overflow with the waves of your infinite tenderness. In this way, may I become a martyr for your Divine Love (Pri 6).

~

God-made-man, your cross is your throne of glory. Your Resurrection is your glorification. Sweep me into your mystery so that I become, through you, a perfect offering of love.

"My time is near....The Son of Man goes as it is written of him" (Mt 26:18–24).

~

After having prepared me to appear before you, if only this martyr could make me finally die so that my soul could leap into the eternal embrace of your merciful love. My Beloved, with each heartbeat, I want to infinitely renew this offering, until such a time when shadows fade and I will be able to tell you again of my love, face to face, eternally! (Pri 6).

~

The final hour for the Son is when humanity is freed from sin. The final hour for humankind is when we are greeted with merciful love so that we can live with grace to the end of the road when we reach the "eternal face to face" with our living God. Lord, prepare me for this meeting.

Holy Thursday

Now before the festival of the Passover, Jesus knew that his hour had come to depart from this world and go to the Father. Having loved his own who were in the world, he loved them to the end (Jn 13:1).

~

At the Last Supper, when Jesus knew his disciples' hearts burned with devoted love after he had just given himself to them through the unfathomable mystery of the Eucharist, this gentle Savior gave them a new commandment. (…) Love one another just as I have loved you (Ms C, 11v).

~

The commandment of charity is founded on the sacrament of love. We can only love one another when we accept the giving of our self. The holy Eucharist is the source of all love. Lord, open my heart to love as you have loved me.

Good Friday

When Jesus knew that all was now finished, he said (in order to fulfill the scripture), "I am thirsty."…When Jesus had received the wine, he said, "It is finished." Then he bowed his head and gave up his spirit (Jn 19:28, 30).

~

The cry of the Lord on the cross, "I am thirsty" sounded continually in my heart....I wanted to give my Beloved a drink, and felt myself devoured by the thirst of all souls.... It was not the souls of priests that attracted me, but those of the big sinners. I burned with the desire to pull them from the eternal flames (Ms A, 45v).

∼

Crucified Jesus, your cry of distress echoes in my heart like a call. You thirst for me to give of myself. Make me aware of your love.

Holy Saturday

There was a garden in the place where he was crucified, and in the garden there was a new tomb in which no one had ever been laid....They laid Jesus there (Jn 19:41–42).

∼

When I saw the blood running from the wounds of Jesus, the thirst of all souls entered my heart. (...) Oh, each day since this special blessing [Pranzini], my desire to save these souls grew. I felt I heard Jesus tell me, "Give me something to drink!" (Ms A, 46v).

∼

Lord, friendly hands laid your wounded body to rest in the tomb. Etch your glorious sainted wounds on my heart.

Easter

Easter Sunday

"Why do you look for the living among the dead? He is not here, but has risen" (Lk 24:5).

~

Celebrations! Even if the most important feasts do not come very often, my heart is brought to celebrate one every Sunday....That is God's feast, the feast of rest.... The whole family goes to Mass (Ms A, 17r).

~

Feast of all feasts—the Sunday of the Resurrection. This is the day when the Church celebrates the Living Eucharist. It is a day of elation and joy. Jesus, you immersed me in your Resurrection on the day of my baptism. May I partake of the peace of children and the rest of the humble, through you, by the sacrament of your Easter.

Easter Monday

So they left the tomb quickly with fear and great joy, and ran to tell his disciples. Suddenly Jesus met them and said, "Greetings!" (Mt 28:8–9).

~

During the Passion of Our Lord, the women showed more courage than the apostles. (...) Undoubtedly, this is why he allowed contempt to be their lot in life on earth, because he chose it for himself....It will be shown, in heaven, that his thoughts were not those of humankind, because the last will be the first (Ms A, 66v).

~

Women with burning hearts, you were the first to receive the news of the Resurrection. Full of joy and emotion, you were the first faithful messengers. Through the gift of your selves, women, you will, without a doubt, always be "the firsts." Lord, let me share these "firsts."

Easter Tuesday

"Do not hold on to me....But go to my brothers and say to them, 'I am ascending to my Father and your Father, to my God and your God'" (Jn 20:17).

~

At times, we are so uncomfortable within ourselves we must quickly reach out. Our Lord doesn't force us to stay within ourselves; oftentimes, he allows us this discomfort so we can reach out. To resolve this, I reach out to Jesus and Mary by throwing myself into acts of charity (CSG 99).

~

It is pointless for me to want to keep God closed within my own little world. Instead, I should stop monopolizing him and reach outside of myself. Lord, make me available to proclaim your Good News and immerse myself in acts of charity in your name.

Easter Wednesday

"Were not our hearts burning within us while he was talking to us on the road, while he was opening the scriptures to us?" That same hour they got up and returned to Jerusalem (Lk 24:32–33).

~

For a long time, I fed my soul with the knowledge of "pure flour" that I found in a book called Imitation. This was the only book I was comfortable with because I had not as yet found the hidden treasures in the Gospel. (...) When I was fourteen, given my interest in knowledge, the Lord found it necessary to combine that "pure flour" with plenty of "oil and honey" (Ms A, 47r).

~

Jesus, you are the heart of the Scriptures. You make me understand the depth of your mystery of love and redemption. May I feed on the nectar of your word so that my life will be filled with the Gospel and shine with your Divine Wisdom.

Easter Thursday

"These are my words that I spoke to you while I was still with you—that everything written about me in the law of Moses, the prophets, and the psalms must be fulfilled." Then he opened their minds to understand the scriptures (Lk 24:44–45).

～

Beloved Sister, how happy we are to understand the intimate secrets of our Divine Spouse! If you would write down all you know of them, we would have some beautiful pages to read. However, you prefer to keep "the secrets of the King" deep within your heart (Ms B, 1v).

～

Secrets are only shared with someone close to you. Jesus, the more I let you teach me, the more you reveal of your heart's secrets: "The only word is that of the Father." I keep your secrets in the silence of my soul as food for contemplation. Nourish my soul.

Easter Friday

"Cast the net to the right side of the boat, and you will find some." So Simon Peter went aboard and hauled the net ashore, full of large fish, a hundred fifty-three of them (Jn 21:6, 11).

~

In spite of my humbleness, I would like to enlighten other souls as did the Prophets and the Doctors of the Church. My vocation is to be an apostle....I want to travel the earth and preach in your name and lift up your glorious cross to the unfaithful. However, my Beloved, I will not be satisfied to do just one such mission. At the same time, I would like to proclaim your Gospel to all corners of the earth, even to the most secluded places (Ms B, 3r).

~

Risen Lord, I must forget myself and be giving so I can be your messenger to the world. I must often cast my nets into uncharted waters. Boldness applied to faith in your Word could have unexpected results. Lord, keep me humble so I can be your messenger.

He appeared to the eleven...and upbraided them for their lack of faith and stubbornness, because they had not believed those who saw him after he had risen. And he said to them, "Go into all the world and proclaim the good news to the whole creation" (Mk 16:14–15).

~

God needs no person to do his divine work. But he does allow a talented gardener to raise exotic and delicate plants by giving him the necessary knowledge but keeping the secret of their creation for himself. In the same way, Jesus wants to be helped in his divine gardening of souls (Ms A, 53r).

~

"Go forth!" Jesus, you ask your disciples to announce the Good News to their own people. Risen Christ, give me a solid enlightened faith so I can be an expression of your Good News.

When it was evening on that day, the first day of the week, and the doors of the house where the disciples had met were locked (...) Jesus came and stood among them and said, "Peace be with you." A week later his disciples were again in the house. (...) Jesus came and stood among them (Jn 20:19–26).

~

This joyous day [Sunday] which passes by all too quickly, has a tinge of sadness....One must start life over again the next day—work, study. My heart feels as if it is in exile on earth....I yearn for eternal rest in heaven, where Sundays never end, in my Father's house (Ms A, 17v).

~

Sunday, the first day of the new world, the eighth day of the world to come in God. Joyous Sundays on earth and never-ending Sundays in heaven! Day of our Risen Lord, celebrated by the Eucharist. A day for people who open themselves to God. It is also the day when God waits for humankind. Lord, make all my days be Sundays!

"The wind blows where it chooses, and you hear the sound of it, but you do not know where it comes from or where it goes. So it is with everyone who is born of the Spirit" (Jn 3:8).

∽

I have carefully prepared myself to receive the Holy Spirit. I could not understand how we don't pay better attention to receiving this sacrament of love [confirmation] (Ms A, 36v).

∽

Through the sacrament of confirmation, I have been particularlyinvigorated by the breath of the Holy Spirit. Spirit of love, rekindle your seven sacred graces in me. Reawaken me to your sacred and enlightening presence.

Second Tuesday of Easter

"Do not be astonished that I said to you, 'You must be born from above.'"…"How can these things be?"…"Are you a teacher of Israel, and yet you do not understand these things?" (Jn 3:7, 9–10).

~

Like the apostles, I eagerly awaited the time when the Holy Spirit would come. I would delight myself at the thought of soon becoming a perfect Christian and, above all, of eternally bearing that mysterious cross, traced on my forehead by the bishop during the sacrament (Ms A, 36v).

~

Holy Spirit, how can we know the realities of heaven without your help? Spirit of light, as I am marked by the sign of victory, help me grasp the redeeming love which the Son of humankind demonstrated on the cross.

Second Wednesday of Easter

For God so loved the world that he gave his only Son…. God did not send the Son into the world to condemn the world, but in order that the world might be saved through him (Jn 3:16–17).

~

The path of love is so gentle. Without question, we may fall, we may be unfaithful, but love can find a way to consume all that could displease Jesus, leaving a single but humble profound peace in our hearts (Ms A, 83r).

~

Father, you showed me the path of love by giving your only Son. Following Jesus, you invite me to take that path of love so I can be free of my infidelities. Let me taste the humble peace of those who have been saved.

Second Thursday of Easter

The one who is of the earth....He whom God has sent speaks the words of God, for he gives the Spirit without measure (Jn 3:31–34).

~

Ever since I understood it was impossible to do anything by myself, the task...no longer appeared difficult. I felt that it was only necessary to unite myself more and more with Jesus and the rest would be given to me as a bonus. In effect, my hope was never mistaken (Ms C, 22v).

~

I am human and only have access to the reality of heaven through you, Jesus. Make me understand it through the Holy Spirit. Be the center of my life. Keep me close to you.

Second Friday of Easter

"There is a boy here who has five barley loaves and two fish...." Then Jesus took the loaves, and when he had given thanks, he distributed them to those who were seated; so also the fish, as much as they wanted (Jn 6:9–11).

~

It isn't enough to give to those who ask, we must anticipate their needs. We must look honored and pleased to be of service. If someone takes something dear to me, I mustn't have any regrets but, on the contrary, appear to be happy to have been rid of it. (...) I am quite far from doing what I understand I must, but just wanting to do it gives me peace (Ms C, 17r).

~

Predicting the wants of those in need and giving something of my own requires generosity. This is not easy but is the only way to know inner peace. Help me give without regrets.

Second Saturday of Easter

His disciples...got into a boat, and started across the sea to Capernaum. It was now dark, and Jesus had not yet come to them. The sea became rough because a strong wind was blowing (Jn 6:16–18).

~

During the joyous days of Easter, Jesus made me aware that there truly were souls without faith. They lose this precious treasure by abusing his blessings. This treasure is a wellspring of only true, pure happiness (Ms C, 5v).

~

For those who abuse the treasure of your blessings, there will only be stormy skies. For those who don't let faith light their way, there will be eternal darkness. For those who let themselves be united with you in faith, there will be true happiness. Christ, let me appreciate your treasures.

Third Sunday of Easter

"Stay with us, because it is almost evening and the day is now nearly over." So he went in to stay with them (Lk 24:29).

~

Jesus, this I know, only love can buy love and as I searched, I found the way to soothe my heart is by giving you my love for your divine love (Ms B, 4r).

~

To be in communion with you, I must invite you to dwell within me. Once we are together in this shared intimacy, you will help me discover your true love. I will have no choice but to respond by giving you my life. Lord, come dwell within me and share your love.

Third Monday of Easter

"Do not work for the food that perishes, but for the food that endures for eternal life, which the Son of Man will give you. For it is on him that God the Father has set his seal" (Jn 6:27).

~

Jesus was the Master, the King....Didn't Thérèse ask him to take away her freedom because it frightened her? She felt so weak and fragile that she wanted to unite herself forever with the divine strength (Ms A, 35r).

~

The life-giving food for everlasting life with you is your body and blood. In exchange, I must also give you my freedom, so that I can find it again, totally reaffirmed in you. This gives me life. Lord, let me have everlasting life in you.

Third Tuesday of Easter

"I am the bread of life. Whoever comes to me will never be hungry, and whoever believes in me will never be thirsty" (Jn 6:35).

~

It seems to me that the Blessed Virgin must have looked at her little flower and smiled at her. Hadn't she healed

her with a simple smile?…Hadn't she laid Jesus, her
Flower of the Field, her Lily of the Valley, in the calyx of
her little flower? (Ms A, 35v).

~

As the chalice on the altar receives your blood, Jesus, so does the flower petal await the morning dew. Let my heart smile in welcome of your resurrected life.

Third Wednesday of Easter

"This is indeed the will of my Father, that all who see the Son and believe in him may have eternal life; and I will raise them up on the last day" (Jn 6:40).

~

Word yet to be created, Word of God!
Oh, you know, I love you, Divine Jesus!
The Spirit of Love embraces me with its fire.
By loving you I attract the Father,
My weak heart keeps him in me without expectation;
Oh Trinity, you are prisoners of my love (PN 17).

~

How could I offer you a fleeting love, faced with your eternal love? Drawn by the Father, my heart is overcome with the Spirit of fire. I will keep you within me to forever share your life of love. Lord, spark my faith.

"No one can come to me unless drawn by the Father who sent me; and I will raise that person up on the last day…. Whoever believes has eternal life" (Jn 6:44–47).

~

To live in love is to give without counting, without seeking return here on earth; oh, I give without measure, being sure that when we love, we do not measure. Divine Heart, overflowing with tenderness, I gave you my all! I run unburdened. I have nothing but my humble treasure which is to live in love (PN 17).

~

Father, I am drawn to you by your love which you show me in your Son. He showed his love without limits, taken to the extreme, so that I could live forever through love. I offer generously of myself, by giving without limits. Lord, let me be generous with my love to you.

"Just as the living Father sent me, and I live because of the Father, so whoever eats me will live because of me" (Jn 6:57).

~

To live in love is to live Your life, glorious King, delight of the chosen! You live for me, hidden in a host. For you, I want to hide myself, Oh Jesus! Lovers need solitude, a heart-to-heart, lasting night and day; your glance alone makes my bliss, I live in your love (PN 17).

~

Living God, I receive abundant life from you. You feed it with the Eucharist. You develop it through the heart-to-heart of prayer. You restore it by your loving glance. Lord, I want to live for you in the secrecy of my heart.

Third Saturday of Easter

"It is the spirit that gives life; the flesh is useless. The words that I have spoken to you are spirit and life" (Jn 6:63).

~

Some of the thoughts of the soul can't be translated into human language without losing their heavenly and intimate meaning. They are like this white stone which will be given to the victor, upon which is written the name no one knows, except the person who receives it (Ms A, 35r).

~

Lord, the way you give me access to myself is only from inside myself, with the enlightenment of your Spirit. My human language can't take me there. May I hear your Word in the privacy of my heart.

Fourth Sunday of Easter

"Very truly, I tell you, I am the gate for the sheep. Whoever enters by me will be saved, and will come in and go out and find pasture" (Jn 10:7, 9).

~

I also feel the desire to love the Lord alone and to find joy only in him (Ms A, 36v).

~

Jesus, you open the path of life to me. You make me appreciate the happiness of living with you. Divine Shepherd, you are the source of my happiness. I tell you over and over of my affection for you. Lord, lead me, your lost sheep, to you always.

Fourth Monday of Easter

"The hired hand runs away because a hired hand does not care for the sheep. I am the good shepherd. I know my own and my own know me, just as the Father knows me and I know the Father" (Jn 10:13–15).

~

To belong to Jesus, one must make oneself small, as small as a dewdrop....Oh, there are very few souls who aspire to stay that small! (...) Jesus made himself like a flower of the field only to show us how much he held simplicity dear. The lily of the valley only hoped to have a small dewdrop (LT 141).

~

Good Shepherd, to you I am worth something. Even as a small lamb, I am dear to you. You know me better that I know myself. Keep my heart simple, listening for your familiar voice.

"My sheep...I give them eternal life and they will never perish. No one will snatch them out of my hand. (…) And no one can snatch them out of the Father's hand" (Jn 10:27–29).

~

Oh, how beautiful is our religion! Instead of shrinking hearts (as the world believes), it lifts them up. It makes them capable of loving with an almost infinite love, since it must continue beyond this mortal life that was given to us, only to reach our heavenly home, where we will once again find those we loved on earth (LT 166).

~

Nothing in your care ever dies. I was made to live in the new world. By the power of your love, I can live through all the events which may occur. I was born to love through you, for all time, all those loved ones that death removes from time. This is my future. Lord, let your love get me through the trying events of my life on earth.

Fourth Wednesday of Easter

"I have come as light into the world, so that everyone who believes in me should not remain in the darkness" (Jn 12:46).

~

I know the country where I live is not my homeland; another is, toward which I must relentlessly aim. (…) It is truly a reality because the King of that shining homeland came to live in this land of darkness for thirty-three years. Alas! The darkness did not understand that this Divine King was the light of the world (Ms C, 5v–6r).

~

Jesus, shining sun, brilliant light, remove me from the darkness of my sins. Clear away the shadows of this world and prepare me to enter the city where you, the Lamb of God, are the shining beacon.

"Very truly, I tell you, servants are not greater than their master, nor are messengers greater than the one who sent them. If you know these things, you are blessed if you do them" (Jn 13:16–17).

~

It is impossible for me to see myself greater than I am because I must see myself as I am, with all my imperfections. But I want to find the way to go to heaven by a straight route, as short as possible, a totally new route (Ms C, 2v).

~

Master, you made yourself a servant. I follow in your footsteps on this totally new route for me, where, to better myself, I must make myself small. I must practice the humble service of messenger, proclaiming the Master. Lord, help me make myself small.

"In my Father's house there are many dwelling places.... Where I am, there you may be also" (Jn 14:2–3).

~

Jesus tells us there are many rooms in our Father's house. If there are rooms for the great souls, for the Fathers of the Desert and for martyrs of punishment, there are surely rooms for little children. Surely, there's a place for us there if we love Jesus, our Heavenly Father and the Spirit of Love (CSG 42).

~

Beyond the value of my love, I already have a place in the heart of God. Each will have their own place at the end of the road, according to the degree of their love. There is no doubt that I will be among the smallest ones, but do not the small ones love with all their hearts? Lord, make room for me in your house.

Fourth Saturday of Easter

"Have I been with you all this time, Philip, and you still do not know me? Whoever has seen me has seen the Father… I am in the Father and the Father is in me" (Jn 14:9–11).

∼

Yes, the Face of Jesus shines. If we consider it beautiful in spite of its wounds and tears, what will it be when we see it in heaven?…Yes, just to have the chance to see the Face of Jesus and contemplate the eternal beauty of Jesus, the poor grain of sand is willing to be scorned on earth (LT 95).

∼

I, your humble grain of sand on the beach of the world, hope to see you, shining Face of God, marvelous vision of beauty. To see you and to know you, to know you so I can love you forever in the contemplation of your Divine Face.

Fifth Sunday of Easter

"I give you a new commandment, that you love one another. Just as I have loved you, you also should love one another. By this everyone will know that you are my disciples, if you have love for one another" (Jn 13:34–35).

∼

I understood that love encompasses all vocations and that love is everything. Love encompasses all times and places.

In a word, it is eternal! Then, in the overabundance of my extraordinary love, I exclaimed, "Oh Jesus, my love...my vocation, I finally found my vocation, it is LOVE*" (Ms B,3v).*

∿

Love is everything since it is giving of oneself totally, all the way to forgiveness. Jesus, you call upon me to love with all the intensity I can, just as you loved us in the abundance of your being. The vocation of all disciples is really love. Lord, let me give my all through love.

Fifth Monday of Easter

"Those who love me will keep my word, and my Father will love them, and we will come to them and make our home with them" (Jn 14:23).

∿

Yes, I can feel it, when I am charitable, it is Jesus working in me. The more I am united with him, the more I love all my sisters (Ms C, 12v).

∿

The more I open myself to you, the more I am intimately joined with you. The more I let you accomplish your work of love in me, the more I live to be in communion with others. This is so because you are the source of all love. Lord, open my heart so I can love others.

Fifth Tuesday of Easter

"Peace I leave with you; my peace I give to you....Do not let your hearts be troubled, and do not let them be afraid" (Jn 14:27).

∿

I have never so well realized the extent of our Lord's kindness and mercy. He sent me this test only when I had the strength to endure it. If he would have sent it earlier, I believe it would have thrown me into despondency. (...) Now, it seems to me, nothing could stop me from soaring as I have no greater desires left except loving until I die of love (Ms C, 7v).

∿

How can someone not be upset, at times frightened, when faced with the harshness of life? If you did not support me with your tender mercy and soothe me with your presence, despondency would set in. Lord, you will always be the one who calms the heart.

Fifth Wednesday of Easter

"You have already been cleansed by the word that I have spoken to you. Abide in me as I abide in you" (Jn 15:3–4).

∿

Our Lord gave me such a faithful heart that when it loved purely, it loved forever (Ms A, 38r).

~

Son of God, by dwelling in me, you tell me what you are: love always faithful, love which transforms. Make me always accept your gift. Keep me united with you in true love.

Fifth Thursday of Easter

"As the Father has loved me, so I have loved you; abide in my love" (Jn 15:9).

~

Jesus doesn't come down from heaven every day just to remain in the golden ciborium. He does it to find another heaven, more precious to him than the first: the heaven of our soul, made in his image, the living temple of the beloved Trinity (Ms A, 48v).

~

Jesus, how deep your love for me must be since it is the same love your Father gave you. You ask me to welcome it and to make my whole being your dwelling place. Blessed Trinity, you bring your mutual love into my heart. Dwell in me, Lord.

"You did not choose me but I chose you. And I appointed you to go and bear fruit, fruit that will last" (Jn 15:16).

～

I feel that, within me, I have the calling to be a priest. How lovingly, Jesus, I would hold you in my hands, when at the sound of my voice, you would come down from heaven....It is with such love, I would give you to the souls! But, alas, while I desire to be a priest, I admire and yearn for the humbleness of Saint Francis of Assisi. I feel the call to do as he did by refusing the sublime dignity of the priesthood (Ms B, 2v).

～

We could be tempted to impose upon you our own view about what is the calling to become a priest, Lord. But it is you who chooses those to be accepted. It is the greatest of ministries, received in humbleness, lived in faith and bearing fruit through love. Lord, show me my true vocation.

Fifth Saturday of Easter

"You do not belong to the world, but I have chosen you out of the world" (Jn 15:19).

~

I did not ignore the fact that, on a trip like the one to Rome, certain things could happen which would upset me. Above all, since I don't know evil, I was afraid that I would find it. I had not experienced that everything is pure to the pure of heart and that a simple and just soul sees no evil. In fact, evil only exists in impure hearts and not in inanimate objects (Ms A, 57r).

~

It is just as harmful to see evil everywhere as it is to see it nowhere. Help me find it, wherever it is. And, since I do not belong to the world, for the time I am here, give me clear vision, a simple heart, and just behavior.

"Love one another as I have loved you. No one has greater love than this, to lay down one's life for one's friends" (Jn 15:12–13).

~

To live in love is to sail forever, spreading seeds of joy and peace in hearts. Beloved Pilot, charity drives me, for I see you in my sisters, the souls. Kindness is my only guiding star. In its light, I sail a straight route, I have my motto written on my sail: "To live in love" (PN 17).

~

To live in love demands that we draw from your spring, Lord. To give one's life presumes that one has lived in love and recognition of others. Your cross, the source and gift of life, is my guiding star to live in love. Lord, guide me.

"When the Advocate comes, whom I will send to you from the Father...he will testify on my behalf. You also are to testify" (Jn 15:26–27).

~

I feel called to the vocation of warrior, of priest, of apostle, of doctor, of martyr; finally, I feel the need, the desire to do it all for you, Jesus, all of the most heroic tasks (Ms B, 2v).

~

How can I testify on your behalf if I am afraid to face life, if I am not sure about the truth, if I am not firm in my convictions? Who would make me strong, but the Advocate, who comes from our Father's side? Strengthen me.

"And when the Advocate comes, he will prove the world wrong about sin and righteousness and judgment: about sin, because they do not believe in me; about righteousness, because I am going to the Father and you will see me no longer; about judgment, because the ruler of this world has been condemned" (Jn 16:8–11).

~

At each new battle, when my enemy comes to provoke me, I am brave, knowing it is cowardly to fight a duel. I turn my back to my adversary without looking him in the face; however, I run toward Jesus. I tell him I'm ready to shed my blood to the very last drop to affirm that there is a heaven (Ms C, 7r).

~

It's wise, not cowardly, to stay away from the enemy because, even if he is condemned, he resorts to trickery, time and time again. Jesus, coming closer to you will help me live the good and proper way, guided by the Spirit. Lord, make me strong in the face of the enemy.

"When the Spirit of truth comes, he will guide you into all the truth....He will glorify me" (Jn 16:13–14).

~

Instead of hurting me, making me vain, the gifts that God lavished upon me (without me even asking), carry me closer to him. I see that it is he alone who is unchanging and only he could fulfill my enormous desires (Ms A, 81v).

~

What I am, I say, I do, and I recognize as truth around me is the result of your work in me, Spirit of truth. Make me seek more truth within myself.

Thursday, Ascension of the Lord

So then the Lord Jesus, after he had spoken to them, was taken up into heaven and sat down at the right hand of God. And they went out and proclaimed the good news everywhere (Mk 16:19–20).

~

Do you know what gives me strength? Well, I work for a missionary. I think that, far away, one of them may be exhausted from his apostolic duties. To reduce his fatigue, I offer mine to the Lord (DE 228) (DE Concordance, varia 2, p. 650).

~

There may be many different ways to proclaim Jesus' Good News but each one has its own part in the mission. For my humble share, my contribution is a conscious gift of the difficult times along my path. Lord, here I am, for you and for the Gospel. Accept my humble gift.

Sixth Friday of Easter

"So you have pain now; but I will see you again, and your hearts will rejoice, and no one will take your joy from you" (Jn 16:22).

~

Oh, how well I know that happiness is not found in the things around us. It is found in the secrecy of the soul. One could have it as well in a prison as in a palace (Ms A, 65r).

~

Pleasure is not true happiness. It is beyond the senses. It is born out of the certainty that you are present in the most intimate parts of myself, at such a depth that surface waves do not reach it. Fruitful Spirit, fill me with your happiness.

Sixth Saturday of Easter

"The Father himself loves you, because you have loved me and have believed that I came from God" (Jn 16:27).

~

My Jesus, I love you. I love the Church, my Mother. I remember that "the smallest act of pure love is more useful to her than all other deeds put together." But is pure love really in my heart?" (Ms B, 4v).

~

Father, according to your Son's teachings, I am sure to be loved by you. In that communion with you, I tell you of my love for Jesus and for his Church. Moreover, only you know the true value of the love that dwells within me. Acknowledge my love.

Seventh Sunday of Easter

"This is eternal life, that they may know you, the only true God, and Jesus Christ whom you have sent" (Jn 17:3).

~

"Life is your vessel, not your dwelling." When I was small, those words gave me courage; even now (...) the image of a vessel still charms my soul and helps it endure exile.... Doesn't Divine Wisdom tell us that "life is like a ship which slices through troubled waters, leaving no trace of its quick passage?" (Ms A, 41r).

~

As a ship at sea, I experience calm waters and both favorable and stormy winds until I arrive at my port. When I will enter your house, I will live in the knowledge you will have given me. Lord, let my ship have smooth sailing on my voyage to your haven.

Seventh Monday of Easter

"In the world you face persecution. But take courage; I have conquered the world!" (Jn 16:33).

~

I am only a child, powerless and weak. However, it is this weakness that gives me the boldness to offer myself as a sacrificial victim to your love, Jesus (Ms B, 3v).

~

I know my fears and weaknesses. But, through you Lord, victorious over sin and death, I draw the strength to give myself to you as an offering of love. Strengthen me.

Seventh Tuesday of Easter

"I have made your name known to those whom you gave me from the world. They were yours, and you gave them to me, and they have kept your word" (Jn 17:6). •

~

The little bird does not grieve over seeing how powerless he is. With bold abandon, he wants to remain fixed on his Divine Sun. Nothing will scare him off, not the wind, nor the rain (Ms B, 5r).

~

In the eyes of humankind, the mission is overwhelming and discouraging. But since I am your possession, Father, and you have given me to your Son, all I have to do is let his penetrating light sweep over me to revive my confidence and energy. Lord, do not let me be overwhelmed.

Seventh Wednesday of Easter

"I have given them your word....Sanctify them in the truth; your word is truth" (Jn 17:14–17).

~

Are my tremendous desires a dream, a fantasy?...Jesus, if they are, make this clear to me; you know I am seeking the truth.... If my desires are foolhardy, make them disappear because, for me, these desires are the greatest of martyrs (Ms B, 4v).

~

To live in the truth is only possible by leaning on you, Jesus. You are the Word of God, the truth in all that is, said, and done. By your Spirit of truth, Lord, guide my search.

Seventh Thursday of Easter

"Father, I desire that those also, whom you have given me, may be with me where I am, to see my glory" (Jn 17:24).

~

I yearn for heaven where we will love Jesus without reservation!...But one must suffer and shed tears to get there....Oh well, I will endure anything that pleases Jesus and let him do what he will with his little toy (LT 79).

~

You want me to always be by your side, where you live in glory. But to get there, I must follow your route, the one of the cross, a path of obedience through love. Lord, keep alive my desire to gaze upon you eternally in your heaven of glory.

Seventh Friday of Easter

Jesus said to Simon Peter, "Simon son of John, do you love me more than these?" He said to him, "Yes, Lord; you know that I love you." Jesus said to him, "Feed my lambs" (Jn 21:15).

∽

I am the child of the Church. (…) Riches and glory are not what the heart of the little child claims. (…) His glory will be the reflection of the glory that will spring from the forehead of his Mother. What he asks for is love….The child knows only one thing, to love you, Jesus (Ms B, 4r).

∽

Oh Church, you are my Mother, born from the rib of Christ in his gesture of love. You are blessed by the Spirit of life. You proceed towards your culmination next to the Father. Holy Church, my Mother, in you, I was born to the Trinitarian life. May I shine like a reflection of your love for the Lord.

"Let anyone who is thirsty come to me, and let the one who believes in me drink. As the scripture has said, 'Out of the believer's heart shall flow rivers of living water.'" Now he said this about the Spirit, which believers in him were to receive (Jn 7:37–39).

～

Mindful of Elisha's prayer to his father Elijah, when he dared to ask him about his dual spirit, I appeared before the angels and saints and said to them, "I am the smallest of humans, I know my misery and weakness. (…) I beg you to adopt me as your child. All the glory you help me gain will be yours alone. (…) I dare to ask you to obtain for me your Love doubled" (Ms B, 4r).

～

Jesus, I pray that faith in you dwells deeply in me and that the supreme gift of the Spirit is bestowed upon me. It will lead me from faith to double love, his love and mine, purified by his. Make me worthy of your love.

Pentecost Sunday

"And I will ask the Father, and he will give you another Advocate, to be with you forever....But the Advocate, the Holy Spirit, whom the Father will send in my name, will teach you everything, and remind you of all that I have said to you" (Jn 14:16–26).

~

Finally, the happy moment [the sacrament of confirmation] arrived. I did not feel a brisk wind when the Holy Spirit descended, but instead, I felt that light breeze on which the Prophet Elijah heard the whisper on Mount Horeb....On that day, I received the strength to suffer (Ms A, 36v).

~

Holy Spirit of God, you took over my heart at my baptism and at my confirmation. You remain forever present in my life. Like a whisper, repeat the words of Jesus to me. Gentle breeze, make these words prolific in me. May your strength keep me brave.

Ordinary Time

First Monday in Ordinary Time

"Follow me and I will make you fish for people." And immediately they left their nets and followed him (Mk 1:17–18).

~

Even though God always asks us to give of ourselves totally, he doesn't come empty-handed. His closest friends have drawn abundantly from his wellspring of strength and courage whenever necessary (Ms A, 51v).

~

"Come" and "follow me"—to these simple words, you add your shining glance of love, your extended hand, burning with tenderness. You hope for an answer from us. Lord, knowing you will always be my source of strength, I am here to do your work.

First Tuesday in Ordinary Time

"A new teaching—with authority! He commands even the unclean spirits, and they obey him" (Mk 1:27).

~

A soul in a state of grace has nothing to fear from the demons who are all cowards and would flee from the mere glance of a child (Ms A, 10v).

~

I have nothing to fear from bad spirits because I am your child. Your glance carries all the strength of your authority and depth of your love. Keep me in your sight.

First Wednesday in Ordinary Time

In the morning, while it was still very dark, he got up and went out to a deserted place, and there he prayed....And he went throughout Galilee, proclaiming the message in their synagogues (Mk 1:35–39).

~

In the early morning, you would come to me and ask if I had given my heart to God. Then you would dress me, speaking of him and after that...I would pray with you....The first word I could read on my own was "heaven" (Ms A, 13v).

~

I offer to you, Lord, this new day as it dawns. I offer it as a gift of your blessing and love. My prayer is one of praise and adoration, but I also listen for your words. Let the Good News fill my day with your presence and love.

First Thursday in Ordinary Time

"If you choose, you can make me clean." Moved with pity, Jesus stretched out his hand and touched him, and said to him, "I do choose. Be made clean!" Immediately the leprosy left him, and he was made clean (Mk 1:40–42).

~

Dear Mother, you were so careful in preparing me [for my first confession] by telling me I was not confessing to a man but that I was going to admit my sins to Our Lord. I was so well convinced of this that I made my confession with a great spirit of faith (Ms A, 16v).

~

To live the sacrament of reconciliation is to present my sinful soul to the purifying power of your love, Lord. It is by receiving this purification with faith that I am restored in your redemptive love. Let me be restored.

First Friday in Ordinary Time

And when they could not bring him to Jesus because of the crowd, they removed the roof above him; and after having dug through it, they let down the mat on which the paralytic lay. When Jesus saw their faith, he said to the paralytic, "Son, your sins are forgiven" (Mk 2:4–5).

~

How light and transparent was the veil which screened Jesus from our sight! Doubt was impossible. Faith and hope were not necessary. Love made us find, here on earth, the One we were seeking (Ms A, 48r).

⁓

Perhaps I should learn to read the tracks that faith leaves along my road. By discovering this expression of love for Christ, I will draw the strength to hope and solidify my own faith. Lord, help me discover your tracks.

First Saturday in Ordinary Time

And as he sat at dinner in Levi's house, many tax collectors and sinners were also sitting with Jesus and his disciples....They said to his disciples, "Why does he eat with tax collectors and sinners?" (Mk 2:15–16).

⁓

I had declared what I was coming to accomplish at Carmel at the foot of Jesus-Eucharist, in the test prior to my profession: "I have come to save souls and above all, pray for the priests." When we want to succeed, we must take the means to do so. Jesus made me understand that it was by the cross that he wanted to give me souls (Ms A, 69v).

⁓

You came to save the sinners by your cross, Lord Jesus. First, redeem me, a poor sinner. And since you invite me to take part in your mission, receive my prayer and penance so that all humanity can be rid of their sins.

Second Sunday in Ordinary Time

"Where are you staying?" He said to them. "Come and see." They came and saw where he was staying, and they remained with him that day (Jn 1:38–39).

~

What will it be when we receive Communion in the eternal kingdom of heaven? (…) His house will be our eternal home….He doesn't want to give us the house that's here on earth. (…) The house he keeps for us is his Palace of Glory. There, we will not see him hidden in the appearance of a child or in a white host, but as he truly is, in the brilliance of his infinite splendor (Ms A, 60r).

~

It is an unforgettable meeting when it allows two people to know one another, to become deeply intimate and remain united. What will it be when you welcome me to your eternal house of glory, Lord? Keep a place for me in your house.

Second Monday in Ordinary Time

"And no one puts new wine into old wineskins; otherwise, the wine will burst the skins, and the wine is lost, and so are the skins; but one puts new wine into fresh wineskins" (Mk 2:22).

～

Lord, I choose it all. I don't want to be a saint halfway. I am not afraid to suffer for you. I am only afraid of one thing, which is to keep my determination. Take it, because, "I choose it all," that is what you want (Ms A, 10v).

～

To live your Good News, Lord, demands that I choose all that is an expression of your will along my path. It will surely be necessary to give up old habits and abandon my will. This is the price I must pay to move ahead in holiness. Lord, help me always choose you and your will.

Second Tuesday in Ordinary Time

One sabbath he was going through the grainfields; and as they made their way his disciples began to pluck heads of grain. The Pharisees said to him, "Look, why are they doing what is not lawful on the sabbath?" (Mk 2:23–24).

～

Yes, all goes well when we only seek Jesus' will. This is why I, a poor little flower, am obedient to Jesus by trying to please my beloved Mother (Ms C, 2v).

～

It is not without destructive consequences to ignore the rules of life. Help me, Lord, to observe these rules, so that I may improve myself by endlessly seeking your will.

Second Wednesday in Ordinary Time

He looked around at them with anger; he was grieved at their hardness of heart and said to the man [with the paralyzed hand], "Stretch out your hand." He stretched it out, and his hand was restored (Mk 3:5).

～

I would like to be ill my whole life if it would please God. I would even agree to a very long life. The only favor I want is that it have interludes of love (Ms C, 8r–v).

~

Lord, a hardened heart will never understand anything about the actions of your love. Only a broken, worn heart is open to your tenderness and mercy. Only you can give me this heart, broken by your love, and filled with compassion for others. Lord, keep my heart open to your blessings.

Second Thursday in Ordinary Time

For he had cured many, so that all who had diseases pressed upon him to touch him (Mk 3:10).

~

Oh Jesus, I beg you to deign to look down on many little souls....I beg you to choose a legion of little victims, worthy of your LOVE! (Ms B, 5v).

~

You could not want such suffering, but you did suffer in your wounded body and in your heart, hurt by sin. You offered the suffering for healing. Lord, touch each one of our hearts so we can share your wounds.

Second Friday in Ordinary Time

He went up the mountain and called to him those whom he wanted, and they came to him. And he appointed twelve, whom he also named apostles, to be with him, and to be sent out to proclaim the message (Mk 3:13–14).

～

Jesus doesn't call souls on the basis of their worth, but calls them as it suits him (Ms A, 2r).

～

You choose your representatives according to your own criteria, given the pressing needs of your Church. You call whom you like, who pleases you, when you see fit. Do you know how disconcerting your methods are for us, for me, Lord? Give me patience and understanding.

Second Saturday in Ordinary Time

When his family heard it, they went out to restrain him, for people were saying, "He has gone out of his mind" (Mk 3:21).

～

Very few souls have not tried to measure divine power in the shortsighted framework of their minds. (...) For a long time, this has been the method humans used to measure life experiences. (...) My Mother, you were not afraid to tell me that God was lighting my soul, and he was even giving me the wisdom of the ages (Ms C, 4r).

∼

The lack of wisdom and experience makes us shortsighted—even when it relates to your action for the kingdom? Lord, make me aware, so I keep the proper perspective.

Third Sunday in Ordinary Time

Jesus came to Galilee, proclaiming the good news of God, and saying, "The time is fulfilled, and the kingdom of God has come near; repent, and believe in the good news" (Mk 1:14–15).

∼

I have had the experience that the soul suffers for a time, even after temporary unfaithfulness. I tell myself then, "My little girl, that is the price you pay for your mistake." I patiently bear it until my small debt is paid (CSG 54).

∼

The Good News of the Gospel can only reach a heart which is open to grace and available to God, acknowledging the consequences of its weaknesses and unfaithfulness. To change is always a grace from God, but one written in a human story. Lord, lead me on the road to change.

Third Monday in Ordinary Time

"And if a house is divided against itself, that house will not be able to stand. And if Satan has risen up against himself and is divided, he cannot stand, but his end has come" (Mk 3:25–26).

~

Holy King David was right when he said: "It is good and kind for people to live together in perfect unison." It's true and I've felt it often; but on earth, this unison must take place amid sacrifice (Ms C, 8v).

~

Living together does not call us to eliminate our differences, but to accept them. These differences only find value through the respect of others and the union of hearts; otherwise, it will divide them. Lord, make me a fraternal person, a uniting force amid a variety of people.

Third Tuesday in Ordinary Time

And looking at those who sat around him, he said, "Here are my mother and my brothers! Whoever does the will of God is my brother and sister and mother" (Mk 3:34–35).

~

My mortifications consisted of breaking my will, which was always ready to impose itself, to hold back a reply, to do little services without noting them, of not resting my back when I sat down, and so on. It is through the practice of little nothings that I prepared myself to be the bride of Jesus (Ms A, 68v).

~

Lord, in order to do your will, I must give up mine, break it. It is a long-term project, through renewed mortifications. I must fulfill that condition to be yours, to work for you. Help me do your will.

Third Wednesday in Ordinary Time

"And these are the ones sown on the good soil: they hear the word and accept it and bear fruit, thirty and sixty and a hundredfold" (Mk 4:20).

~

The poor little flower had been accustomed to digging her fragile roots into chosen soil, made especially for her. It was difficult for it to find itself in the midst of all kinds of flowers [at boarding school], with their often uncaring roots, to be forced to find its necessary nourishment for survival in the communal soil (Ms A, 22r).

~

Whether you planted me in chosen soil or difficult terrain, today you place me, a delicate plant, in the midst of dense vegetation. You invite me to live there and dig deeper to find the nourishment of your presence and blessings which will help me bear your fruit. Lord, nourish my roots.

Third Thursday in Ordinary Time

"The measure you give will be the measure you get, and still more will be given you. For to those who have, more will be given" (Mk 4:24–25).

~

Upon meditating on the words of Jesus, I understood just how imperfect my love for my sisters was. I saw that I didn't love them the same way Our Lord did. Oh, now I understand that perfect charity is comprised of enduring others' faults, not being surprised by their weaknesses, and being happy to see them do even the smallest acts of virtue (Ms C, 12r).

~

A good gauge is fraternal love which makes me look at others without judgment and discover in them, without surprise, beauty and goodness, as well as faults and weakness. It is an evaluation done in love. Lord, may I love others in your way.

"The kingdom of God is as if someone would scatter seed on the ground, and would sleep and rise night and day, and the seed would sprout and grow, he does not know how" (Mk 4:26–27).

Just as the sun shines at the same time on trees and flowers, like each was the only one on earth, so does our Lord care for all souls in a special manner, as if they were each unique (Ms A, 3r).

Lord, when I look across your fields, I see a variety of trees, plants, and different kinds of vegetation. And I would like to change them, make them all the same! But no, everything grows in you, each in its own way. Whether I am a towering tree or the humblest of flowers, it is not important, as long as I am gifted with your blessings, and grow in you. Bless me, help me grow in you.

Third Saturday in Ordinary Time

He said to them, "Why are you afraid? Have you still no faith?" (Mk 4:40).

~

There is only one thing to do during the unique night which comes but once in a lifetime. It is to love, to love Jesus with all the strength of our heart and to save souls so that he will be loved (LT 96).

~

All nights, nights of faith, nights in life, the eve of our death, produce fear. Jesus, how can we wait for the light of day, if not through faith in you, love for you, and with the certainty of your love for me? Love chases the night away. Lord, ease my fears.

Fourth Sunday in Ordinary Time

And when the sabbath came, he entered the synagogue and taught. They were astounded at his teaching, for he taught them as one having authority (Mk 1:21–22).

~

Sometimes, I would try to fish with my small line but I preferred to go sit alone among the flowers. At those times, I had deep thoughts without even knowing I was meditating, and my soul plunged into genuine prayer....I heard sounds from far away....The earth felt like a place of exile and I dreamed of heaven (Ms A, 14v).

⁓

Lord, you don't fail to teach me, through the work of your creation, through the message of your Gospel, or through the open book of your cross. Teacher of truth, when I withdraw into silence, you reach me. Then, everything becomes a prayer. Lord, always teach me.

Fourth Monday in Ordinary Time

"Go home to your friends, and tell them how much the Lord has done for you, and what mercy he has shown you" (Mk 5:19).

⁓

Oh, how quickly the sunny years of my childhood went by! But what a gentle imprint they have left on my soul (Ms A, 11v).

⁓

Lord, you have left numerous imprints on my soul. You let me discover them so I can be amazed at you, at your work in me, and so that I can proclaim the tenderness and mercy you have shown me. You are right to invite me to search my soul so I can discover you. Lord, guide my search.

Now there was a woman who had been suffering from hemorrhages for twelve years....She had heard about Jesus, and came up behind him in the crowd and touched his cloak....Immediately aware that power had gone forth from him, Jesus turned about in the crowd and said, "Who touched my clothes?" (Mk 5:25, 27, 30).

~

Our Dear Lord saw fit to submit my soul to many types of hardship. I have suffered a great deal on earth. But, while I suffered in sadness as a child, that's not how I suffer now. I suffer in joy and peace. I am truly happy to suffer (Ms C, 4v).

~

Hardship is a part of life, but when it continues, how can we withstand it? How can we not get angry at God and cry out in dismay? Lord Jesus, we need to draw strength from you to be able to suffer in joy and in peace. Perhaps I should know rejection and sadness before I call for that strength. Lord, I am ready to suffer as you see fit.

Fourth Wednesday in Ordinary Time

On the sabbath he began to teach in the synagogue, and many who heard him were astounded. They said, "Where did this man get all this? What is this wisdom that has been given to him?...Is not this the carpenter, the son of Mary?" (Mk 6:2–3).

~

Often, they praise the intelligence of others in front of me, but never mine. Thus, I have concluded I have none, and resigned myself to be deprived of it (Ms A, 38r).

~

I can be jealous or resentful of the intelligence of others, but what good is that? I am filled with wonder by your teachings and wisdom. Your words as a man open us to your life as the Son of God. I have much to learn.

He called the twelve and began to send them out two by two. (...) He ordered them..."Wherever you enter a house, stay there until you leave the place" (Mk 6:7–10).

~

In going over all you have told me [about the life at Carmel], I felt that Carmel was the desert where God wanted me to hide....This was not a foolish childhood dream, but the certainty of a divine calling. I wanted to go to Carmel, not for Pauline [my sister], but only for Jesus (Ms A, 26r).

~

Throughout the history of the Church, you have never stopped calling people to do your mission. But Lord, to take on your mission, one must spend days in the desert alone with you, as well as moments of fraternal sharing and hours of joy in the hospitality of humankind. I want my life to be dedicated to you alone, within the limits of my own spiritual and human capabilities. Lord, call me to your mission.

Herod said to the girl, "Ask me for whatever you wish, and I will give it."...She rushed back to the king and requested, "I want you to give me at once the head of John the Baptist on a platter."...Immediately the king sent a soldier of the guard with orders to bring John's head (Mk 6:22, 25, 27).

～

Oh, truly everything smiled upon me on earth. I found flowers wherever I stepped...but a new era was beginning for my soul. I would have to go through the test of hardship and suffering, beginning as early on as my childhood, so I could be offered sooner to Jesus (Ms A, 12r).

～

At times, it may cost us everything to be faithful to the mission and defend the truth. Good times, which give us courage, are followed by trying times, where God is there but hidden. Lord, give me courage to find you each hour.

The apostles gathered around Jesus, and told him all that they had done and taught. He said to them, "Come away to a deserted place all by yourselves and rest a while" (Mk 6:30–31).

～

One of the teachers at the Abbey asked me what I did on my days off, when I was alone. I replied that I went to an empty space behind my bed which I could easily close with a curtain, and there I thought….But what do you think about?…I think about God, about life…about eternity, in short, I just think! I now understand I was praying (Ms A, 33v).

～

It is truly necessary and beneficial to spend time in silence, away from the turbulence of life, where I can then ponder about the important things and join with you, Lord, to assume my life in you. To me, praying is just this: to retire in silence and to be received in your heart. Lord, lead me to that quiet place of prayer.

Fifth Sunday in Ordinary Time

In the morning, while it was still very dark, he got up and went out to a deserted place, and there he prayed. And Simon and his companions hunted for him. When they found him, they said to him, "Everyone is searching for you" (Mk 1:35–37).

~

Oh, how sweet is the way of love!...Oh, how I wish to always do the will of God with no restraints (Ms A, 84v).

~

Lord, to look for you I must already be on the way of love. I must have given up my creature comforts, stood up, and quieted my conflicts. It will be an easy road if I do your will and not my own. Lord, help me do your will.

Fifth Monday in Ordinary Time

When they had crossed over, they came to land at Gennesaret and moored the boat. When they got out of the boat, people at once recognized him (Mk 6:53–54).

~

[In Trouville]—I will never forget the impression the sea made upon me. I couldn't stop looking at it: its majesty, the roaring of its waves. It all spoke to my soul of the grandeur and the power of God (Ms A, 21v).

~

The Sea of Galilee, sometimes calm, sometimes tumultuous, is enchanting and impressive. We do not tire of admiring its waves and vastness, its life and mystery. Bless the Lord for the seas and all that live in theirf waters.

Fifth Tuesday in Ordinary Time

"You have a fine way of rejecting the commandment of God in order to keep your tradition!…But you…void the word of God through your tradition that you have handed on" (Mk 7:9–13).

~

I understood that only love made the members of the Church act. If love died, the apostles would no longer

proclaim the Good News and the martyrs would refuse
to shed their blood (Ms B, 3v).

~

When our customs are no longer representative of our human condition or our spiritual life, we either suppress them or give them a new breath of life. If my actions toward God are no longer expressions of deep love, what are my actions worth? Make my actions always expressive of love.

Fifth Wednesday in Ordinary Time

"Do you not see that whatever goes into a person from outside cannot defile, since it enters, not the heart but the stomach, and goes out into the sewer?…For it is from within, from the human heart, that evil intentions come…. All these evil things come from within" (Mk 7:18, 19, 21, 23).

~

I didn't know how to play, but I loved to read and would have gladly spent my life at it. Fortunately, I had earthly angels around me to guide my choice of books, amusing me while nourishing my heart and spirit….God never allowed a harmful book to reach me (Ms A, 31v).

~

Reading is as necessary to my spirit as food is to my body. It is up to me to choose the food for my mind wisely, because the point of origin for my conscious deeds is my heart, my inner self. Lord, guard me against those things which may hurt me.

Fifth Thursday in Ordinary Time

Now the woman...begged him to cast the demon out of her daughter. He said to her, "Let the children be fed first, for it is not fair to take the children's food and throw it to the dogs." But she answered him, "Sir, even the dogs under the table eat the children's crumbs." Then he said to her, "For saying that, you may go—the demon has left your daughter" (Mk 7:26–29).

∼

As in nature, where all the seasons are arranged in such a way that the humblest daisy blossoms on its appointed day, it is exactly the same for each soul (Ms A, 3r).

∼

Lord, even if the littlest dogs are not forgotten, it goes without saying that you will take care of the humblest of your children. But, on the appointed day, you give out your blessings when your child becomes capable of receiving your gift, when his prayers are not only requests but pleas of faith.

Then looking up to heaven, he sighed and said to him, "Ephphatha," that is, "Be opened." And immediately his ears were opened, his tongue was released, and he spoke plainly (Mk 7:34–35).

~

Jesus, I can't even begin to tell the little souls just how beyond words your condescension is....As impossible as it seems, I feel that if you should find a weaker soul than mine, you would happily give it larger favors if it gave itself, in total confidence, to your infinite mercy (Ms B, 5v).

~

Jesus, you take into consideration all calls of distress. When you find a weak and fragile being before you asking for help, you open them to love by opening them to life, through the power of your breath of creation. You will always be the closest one. Lord, hear my call.

"I have compassion for the crowd, because they have been with me now for three days and have nothing to eat. If I send them away hungry to their homes, they will faint on the way" (Mk 8:2–3).

~

When I want to rest my tired heart from the darkness which surrounds it, I think of that bright and shining place where I hope to go and my agony doubles. It seems to me that the darkness (...) says to me: "You dream of the light, (...) the eternal possession of the Creator. (...) Go forward, be happy with the death that will give you, not what you hope for, but (...) the night of nothingness" (Ms C, 6v).

~

Isn't it enough to make you falter along the way when the road becomes dark like a night of nothingness, instead of being lit and full of hope? My dream of light and possession of you is nevertheless not ridiculous, because your words echo deeply inside me, "I have compassion." Lord, make my dream come true.

Sixth Sunday in Ordinary Time

A leper came to him begging him, and kneeling he said to him, "If you choose, you can make me clean" (Mk 1:40).

～

I can ask nothing more with earnestness than the perfect fulfillment of God's will for my soul, without anything on earth standing in its way (Ms A, 83r).

～

When illness crushes us, how can we not ask for relief through prayer? But you will only answer, "if you so wish." I am not sure I understand your will, Lord, but I leave my future in your hands.

The Pharisees came and began to argue with him, asking him for a sign from heaven, to test him. And he sighed deeply in his spirit and said, "Why does this generation ask for a sign? Truly I tell you, no sign will be given to this generation" (Mk 8:11–12).

~

May Jesus forgive me if I caused him sorrow. But he knows that while I don't have the delight of faith, I endeavor at least to do its work. I believe I have done more acts of faith in the past year than I have done during my entire life before that (Ms C, 7r).

~

The signs to help me believe come under many guises and can support me along the road to faith. However, I will often have to continue ahead in the darkness of faith and transfer into myself, and by my way of life, the fact that you, Risen Christ, are the heart of my existence and my reason for continuing. Lord, calm my fear of the darkness when faith seems far removed.

"Are your hearts hardened? Do you have eyes, and fail to see? Do you have ears, and fail to hear? And do you not remember?...Do you not yet understand?" (Mk 8:17–18, 21).

~

[Jesus] allowed the darkest shadows to take over my soul and thus, my sweet thoughts of heaven became nothing but cause for struggle and torment. (...) This hardship would only end at the time determined by God. (...) One must have traveled through that dismal tunnel to fully understand its darkness (Ms C, 5v).

~

A cloudy horizon, dark places, closed hearts, all do exist. To stop then would be harmful. I must push forward without completely understanding or knowing the length of that dark tunnel. Lord, when you decide the time is right, light will come.

Then Jesus laid his hands on his eyes again; and he looked intently and his sight was restored, and he saw everything clearly (Mk 8:25).

~

I feel powerless to use human language to repeat the secrets of heaven. (...) There are so many different horizons and infinitely varied nuances. Only the palette of the Heavenly Painter can give me, after my death, the necessary colors to paint the marvels he unveils to my soul (Ms B, 1v).

~

In the full light of day, creation reveals the splendor of its nuances to me. What will it be like when, in the light of Christ, I will see God and his marvels among the chosen ones? At that time, I will see everything clearly.

Then he began to teach them that the Son of Man must undergo great suffering, and be rejected by the elders, the chief priests, and the scribes, and be killed, and after three days rise again (Mk 8:31).

~

Martyrdom, that's my childhood dream. That dream has grown with me in the cloisters of Carmel....But there again, I feel that my dream is a fantasy because I could not limit myself to want just one type of martyrdom.... For me to be satisfied, I would need to have them all (Ms B, 3r).

~

I wouldn't presume to dream of becoming a martyr, Lord. It can only be a special calling from you, with the help of your blessing. Your crucifixion was your martyrdom, your testimony of love. In the Church, my baptism and confirmation made me a witness. Help my dreams become a reality in my life.

Sixth Friday in Ordinary Time

"If any want to become my followers, let them deny themselves and take up their cross and follow me" (Mk 8:34).

~

It seems to me if you found souls offered as sacrificial victims to your love, you would quickly consume them. (...) If your divine justice, which only extends to earth, likes to unburden itself, then how much more your benevolent love must yearn to embrace the souls, since your mercy rises all the way to heaven! Oh Jesus, (...) consume your sacrificial victim by the fire of your divine love" (Ms A, 84r).

~

You call me to march onward, Lord, when at times, renunciation and crosses slow me down. This walk is only possible when I lean on your tenderness, supported by your mercy. You await the offering of my whole being to energize my walk with the consuming fire of your love. Lord, have mercy.

Jesus…was transfigured before them, and his clothes became dazzling white, such as no one on earth could bleach them (Mk 9:2–3).

~

Why don't you keep these immense desires for (…) the eagles who soar to great heights? Me, I consider myself only a weak little bird. (…) I am not an eagle, I only have the eyes and the heart of an eagle. In spite of my extreme smallness, I dare gaze at the Divine Sun, the Sun of Love. My heart feels, within itself, all the desires of the eagle (Ms B, 4v–5r).

~

Lord Jesus, you are a fascinating sight for the eyes who look into the depth of faith, and for the heart that is lifted to the heights of love. The desires of the majestic dwell in my weakness. You made me for the fullness of love.

Seventh Sunday in Ordinary Time

Some people came, bringing to him a paralyzed man, carried by four of them. And when they could not bring him to Jesus because of the crowd, they removed the roof above him; and after having dug through it, they let down the mat on which the paralytic lay. When Jesus saw their faith, he said to the paralytic, "Son, your sins are forgiven" (Mk 2:3–5).

~

I was really too bold!...Happily, God who sees into the depth of our hearts, knows that my intentions were pure. He knows that I would not want to displease him for anything in the world (Ms A, 66v).

~

Boldness could lead to recklessness, unless it is an expression of a deep and generous faith or unfailing confidence in the Lord. Give me the boldness of faith and assurance in you so that I can help my brothers and sisters discover and welcome your liberating gifts.

"But if you are able to do anything, have pity on us and help us."..."All things can be done for the one who believes."..."I believe; help my unbelief!" (Mk 9:22–24).

~

[The veil of faith] is a wall that reaches all the way to the heavens. (…) When I sing of (…) the eternal possession of God, I feel no joy because I simply sing what I WANT TO BELIEVE. *Sometimes (…) a tiny ray of sunshine comes to shed light on my gloom. Then, this trial stops for a moment but afterwards, instead of giving me joy, the memory of that ray makes my gloom even thicker (Ms C, 7v).*

~

Along the path of faith, we could meet a wall that may appear insurmountable. "If you could do something... come" is the only sound that could arise out of my heart. Lord, if the gloom remains, make me want to believe in spite of the impossible.

Seventh Tuesday in Ordinary Time

"Whoever wants to be first must be last of all and servant of all" (Mk 9:35).

~

I was not satisfied just to pray for the sister who gave me so many battles. I tried to do all the favors I possibly could for her. When I was tempted to reply in a disagreeable way, I would just give her my most loving smile and try to change the subject (Ms C, 14r).

~

It is better to appreciate other people than to be appreciated by them. This requires a charitable attitude, courteous conversation, a victory over ourselves. These are attitudes I must adopt to be the first among the humble. Lord, help me have such an attitude towards others.

Seventh Wednesday in Ordinary Time

"For no one who does a deed of power in my name will be able soon afterward to speak evil of me. Whoever is not against us is for us" (Mk 9:39–40).

~

For a long time, I have asked myself, why (…) all souls don't receive an equal amount of blessings….He [Jesus] put the book of nature before me and I understood that all of the flowers he created are beautiful (Ms A, 2r–v).

~

It is always risky to classify others as "for" or "against." What do I know about the hearts of others? Rather, I should try to discover the beauty in others like reflections of blessings. Each person has his or her own measure of blessings. Lord, make me appreciate the beauty in all of your creations.

Seventh Thursday in Ordinary Time

"For truly I tell you, whoever gives you a cup of water to drink because you bear the name of Christ will by no means lose the reward" (Mk 9:41).

~

Merit does not consist of doing or giving a great deal, but rather in receiving and loving a great deal. It is said that it is better to give than to receive, that's true, but when Jesus wants to take the sweetness of giving for himself, it would not be gracious to refuse (LT 142).

~

A heart that loves is more precious than what it gives. A heart that gives could only be filled with love. A heart that receives, welcomes the expression of love. Lord, for you, I want to be giving. Make me welcome your gracious gifts.

Seventh Friday in Ordinary Time

"From the beginning of creation, 'God made them male and female. For this reason a man shall leave his father and mother and be joined to his wife, and the two shall become one flesh.' So they are no longer two, but one flesh" (Mk 10:6–8).

~

During my retreat, I realized that I was a cherished and protected child, as there are very few on earth, especially among those who have lost their mother (Ms A, 34r).

~

Man and woman are joined as one when they form a couple, bearers of life, love, and knowledge. This was God's will for always. Happy are the couples who live the will of God. Happy are the cherished children.

Seventh Saturday in Ordinary Time

People were bringing little children to him in order that he might touch them;…And he took them up in his arms, laid his hands on them, and blessed them (Mk 10:13–16).

~

God offered me the solace of observing children's souls. I understood what a misfortune it was not to mold them from their very first moments of awareness when they are like soft wax on which one can imprint both virtues as well as evil....Oh, how many souls would make it to holiness if only they were well guided (Ms A, 52v–53r).

～

A little child's heart is like new soil in which we must plant humanity and let God plant his own seeds of life. Lord Jesus, help parents, teachers, and catechists fulfill their mission with the children.

Eighth Sunday in Ordinary Time

"No one sews a piece of unshrunk cloth on an old cloak; otherwise, the patch pulls away from it, the new from the old, and a worse tear is made" (Mk 2:21).

～

Illusions...God blessed me by giving me NONE *when I entered Carmel. I found that religious life was just as I had imagined. (...) At the beginning, I stepped on more thorns than roses!...Suffering reached out to me and I threw myself into it with love (Ms A, 69v).*

～

Giving oneself to God is entering into a new life that requires no repair because God is the fountain of eternal youth. No illusions! One must give up the old habit of one's inner self and live a life of mutual support so that the roses may flower. Lord, may I have no illusions.

Eighth Monday in Ordinary Time

"You lack one thing; go, sell what you own, and give the money to the poor, and you will have treasure in heaven; then come, follow me." When he heard this, he was shocked and went away grieving, for he had many possessions (Mk 10:21–22).

~

In my thoughts, I like to return to those enchanted places where my worldly friends lived…to ask myself where they are now and what they get from the comforts of life they have in their castles and parks. I see that all of it is vanity. (…) The only worthy possession is to love God with all our heart and to be here on earth, poor in spirit (Ms A, 32v).

~

If it is only given to a few to sacrifice all their worldly goods, then detachment from material goods is within reach for us all through poverty of spirit in order to love the One in truth. What must I give up? Lord, guide me.

Eighth Tuesday in Ordinary Time

Peter began to say to him, "Look, we have left everything and followed you" (Mk 10:28).

~

How I thank Jesus for making me find only bitterness in my friendships on earth! With a heart like mine, I would have let myself be taken in and had my wings clipped. Then, how could I have flown and rested? (Ms A, 38r).

⁓

Lord, you ask some "to give everything up to follow you," to live the wealth of being for you, not to isolate themselves, but to go out and bring their brothers and sisters to the heights of love. Lord, protect their gift.

Eighth Wednesday in Ordinary Time

"The cup that I drink you will drink; and with the baptism with which I am baptized, you will be baptized" (Mk 10:39).

⁓

The day after my first Communion (...) I felt a great desire to suffer come to life in my heart. At the same time, I was assured that Jesus was keeping many crosses for me to bear. I felt flooded with such great solace that I consider it one of the greatest blessings of my life (Ms A, 36r).

⁓

When I receive your body and blood in Communion, I am pledged to enter into the mystery of your death through daily crosses, to emerge alive with your life. Lord, help me to grasp the extent to which holy Communion supports me.

Bartimaeus son of Timaeus, a blind beggar, was sitting by the roadside….He began to shout out and say, "Jesus, Son of David, have mercy on me!"…Then Jesus said to him, "What do you want me to do for you?" The blind man said to him, "My teacher, let me see again." Jesus said to him, "Go; your faith has made you well" (Mk 10:46–47, 51–52).

~

I want to suffer out of love and even enjoy out of love. In this way, I will throw flowers before your throne. (…) I will sing even when I must pick my flowers amid thorns. The longer and sharper the thorns are, the sweeter my song will sound (Ms B, 4v).

~

Son of David, perhaps I will have to sit for a long time at the side of the road, crying out in distress before I hear your voice. Perhaps you want to force me to discover for myself that flowers are entangled with the thorns of suffering. Lord, if I do not see them, may I at least feel them.

Jesus answered them, "Have faith in God. Truly I tell you, if you say to this mountain, 'Be taken up and thrown into the sea,' and if you do not doubt in your heart, but believe that what you say will come to pass, it will be done for you" (Mk 11:22–23).

~

I have always wanted to be a saint. But, alas, I always realized when I compared myself to the saints, that the differences between us were as great as those between a mountain peak hidden by clouds and a single grain of sand underfoot to those passing by (Ms C, 2v).

~

I sometimes create a mountain out of a single grain of sand along my path. I am afraid to climb the mountains that would bring me closer to you. Lord, give me the strength of love so that I can level these paths of sand, and the passion of faith to reach the peak of holiness.

As he was walking in the temple, the chief priests, the scribes, and the elders came to him and said, "By what authority are you doing these things? Who gave you this authority to do them?" (Mk 11:27–28).

~

Oh how humans are so shortsighted!…Whenever we see someone who is more enlightened by the faith, we jump to the conclusion that Jesus loves us less and we could never be called to that same level of perfection. Since when has the Lord no right to use one of his humans to give out the necessary food to the souls he loves? (Ms C, 19v–20r).

~

Lord, sometimes I question you as if I had authority over you and as if you have to answer to me. These are the empty claims and shortsightedness of humans. You give each of us what we need and by these different choices, you carry out your work in our hearts. Keep me available to do your will.

"Is it lawful...on the sabbath, to save life or to kill?" But they were silent. He looked around at them with anger; he was grieved at their hardness of heart and said to the man, "Stretch out your hand." He stretched it out, and his hand was restored (Mk 3:4–5).

~

After I joined Pauline, I made up my mind to never keep my soul too far away from the sight of Jesus, so that it sails in peace towards our home in heaven (Ms A, 22r).

~

What a deep disappointment it is when faced with loving behavior, one fails to understand and turns away! What happiness when two glances meet and understand each other! Jesus, put me face to face with love for you.

"Then he sent another [servant], and that one they [the wine growers] killed. And so it was with many others….He had still one other, a beloved son. Finally he sent him to them, saying, 'They will respect my son.' So they seized him, killed him, and threw him out of the vineyard" (Mk 12:5–6, 8).

∼

He, whose kingdom is not of this world, showed me that true wisdom consists of "wanting to be ignored and counted as having little value" and of "putting one's happiness in the scorn of one's self."…As that of Jesus, I would like "my face to be truly hidden so that no one on earth recognizes me." I thirst to suffer and be forgotten (Ms A, 71r).

∼

If the wine growers did not recognize you as the Son, it is because you remain a hidden God. You will only reveal yourself as the God of Glory at the end of the road. To be lost in the crowd but recognized by you in love, Lord, from now on, that is what matters to me.

"Teacher, we know that you are sincere, and show deference to no one; for you do not regard people with partiality, but teach the way of God in accordance with truth" (Mk 12:14).

～

It seems to me that if all humans have the same blessings as me, God would not be feared by anyone but loved immensely. (…) I understand, however, that all souls cannot be alike. There must be different groups to particularly honor each one of God's perfections (Ms A, 83v).

～

You don't differentiate between your people, yet you created them to be different. Lord, each of us shows traces of you. By pooling our differences, we reveal the diversity of your gifts. Help me respect each person for what they are.

Ninth Wednesday in Ordinary Time

"For when they rise from the dead, they neither marry nor are given in marriage, but are like angels in heaven" (Mk 12:25).

〜

Beloved Eagle, one day, I hope you will come get your little bird and, taking it up to your hearth of love, you will immerse it for eternity, into the burning abyss of that love, to which it offered itself as a victim (Ms B, 5v).

〜

Keeping myself for you alone leads to offering myself, day after day, and being consumed in your love. I wait to be introduced to your abyss of love, to be transformed into a new world, living the same communion of the saints. Lord, show me the abyss of love.

Ninth Thursday in Ordinary Time

"The first [commandment] is…'you shall love the Lord your God.' The second is this, 'You shall love your neighbor as yourself.' There is no other commandment greater than these" (Mk 12:29–31).

〜

This year, God gave me the blessing to be able to under-
stand the meaning of charity. Before then, I understood
it, (...) but in an imperfect way. I hadn't studied this
teaching of Jesus in depth: 'the second commandment is
SIMILAR *to the first: love your neighbor as yourself' (Ms*
C, 11v).

~

The source for the second commandment is the first. The
partial expression of the first is the second. Partial, because
I love you, Lord, for yourself. I love myself through you. I
love my neighbor because of you. Make me understand
that this is charity.

Ninth Friday in Ordinary Time

"How can the scribes say that the Messiah is the son of
David?...David himself calls him Lord; so how can he be
his son?" And the large crowd was listening to him with
delight (Mk 12:35–37).

~

[Mother,] my inexperience and youth didn't bother you.
Perhaps you remembered that our Lord often liked to give
wisdom to the children, and that one day, moved by joy,
he blessed his Father for having hidden his secrets from
the sages and revealing them to the children (Ms C, 4r).

~

You confuse the minds of those who boast of their knowledge. You enlighten those who examine your mystery with a simplicity of heart. You are moved with joy by those who listen to you with pleasure. Lord, give me a simple heart that listens.

Ninth Saturday in Ordinary Time

"This poor widow has put in more than all those who are contributing to the treasury. For all of them have contributed out of their abundance; but she out of her poverty has put in everything she had, all she had to live on" (Mk 12:43–44).

~

To give to all those who ask is less sweet than offering oneself by an act of the heart. When we are asked kindly, giving seems to cost nothing. But if by misfortune, one doesn't use kind words, immediately the soul would rebel if it isn't convinced of its charity (Ms C, 15v).

~

To give of what one has is already commendable. To give of what one is, is a commitment. The more spontaneous the gift is, the truer it is. Again, I must respect others so as not to humiliate them. Lord, may I give spontaneously, without being asked.

Tenth Sunday in Ordinary Time

As Jesus was walking along, he saw a man called Matthew sitting at the tax booth; and he said to him, "Follow me." And he got up and followed him (Mt 9:9).

~

This desire [to become a great saint] could seem fool-hardy if one considers just how weak and imperfect I was and still am after seven years of religious life. Nevertheless, I still feel the same bold confidence in becoming a great saint because I don't rely upon my merits, as I have none, but I put my hope in He who is virtue and saintliness itself (Ms A, 32r).

~

You take me no matter where I am on my route, to make me into someone according to your heart. You call me to follow in your steps, filled with the desire for sainthood. Beyond my weaknesses and imperfections, Lord, be my strength and confidence.

Tenth Monday in Ordinary Time

"Blessed are the poor in spirit, for theirs is the kingdom of heaven....Blessed are the pure in heart, for they will see God" (Mt 5:3–8).

∽

Finally, my desires were fulfilled [upon my entrance to Carmel]. My soul felt a PEACE so gentle and so deep it would be impossible to express it. For the past seven-and-a-half years, this intimate peace remained with me. It never abandoned me, even in the midst of the greatest trials (Ms A, 69r–v).

∽

True happiness does not entail intense excitement, but indescribable inner peace. It remains in spite of the hazards in life. Lord, give me a heart wishing simple and straightforward happiness.

Tenth Tuesday in Ordinary Time

"You are the salt of the earth; but if salt has lost its taste, how can its saltiness be restored? It is no longer good for anything, but is thrown out and trampled under foot"(Mt 5:13).

∽

When one does what one must, never making excuses, it goes unnoticed. On the other hand, imperfections show right away….Above all, I apply myself to practice the small virtues. (…) [Penance] granted to me without my asking only mortifies my ego. That was better for me than corporal penance (Ms A, 74v).

~

How can one have a taste for life if not by being true to oneself, working to correct deficiencies, and refusing all attitudes of superiority. Lord, make me a stimulating component in the Church.

Tenth Wednesday in Ordinary Time

"Do not think that I have come to abolish the law or the prophets; I have come not to abolish but to fulfill" (Mt 5:17).

~

Oh, if all of the weak and imperfect souls felt the same way as the smallest of all souls, that of your little Thérèse, not a single one of them would lose hope to reach the summit of the mountain of love. Jesus doesn't ask us to do big things, only self-abandonment and gratitude (Ms B, 1v).

~

If we have to take a winding road to reach the peak of the mountain, I have to walk even more along paths of self-abandon, leaning on the climbing pick of the commandments to reach the peak of love which is the fulfillment in Christ. Lord, help me climb to the top.

Tenth Thursday in Ordinary Time

"Come to terms quickly with your accuser while you are on the way to court with him" (Mt 5:25).

~

Each time I met her [the sister who displeased me in everything], I prayed to God for her; offering him all of her merits and virtues. I felt that this pleased Jesus. (...) Jesus, artist of the souls, is happy when we don't stop at the outer layer, but delve deeper, right to the inner core of the soul, where Jesus has chosen to live, and where we can admire its beauty (Ms C, 14r).

~

When I look closely at my neighbor, it may menace and annoy them. If I go beyond the outer layer, if I realize that every being is, in some way, your home, Lord, then I will be able to praise and admire you in others. Help me to look beyond the surface.

Tenth Friday in Ordinary Time

"It is better for you to lose one of your members [limbs] than for your whole body to go into hell" (Mt 5:30).

~

God gave me the grace to know the world just enough to despise it and push it away. (...) At the age of ten, a heart can be easily dazzled. I find it was a great blessing to have not stayed in Alençon (Ms A, 32v).

~

To remain faithful, faced with the proposals of a confused world, one must practice good judgment. It is so easy to be dazzled. Lord, give me perception and courage when faced with a difficult decision.

Tenth Saturday in Ordinary Time

"Let your word be 'Yes, Yes' or 'No, No'; anything more than this comes from the evil one" (Mt 5:37).

~

If one says something unfair to you, or if a Sister, who is not knowledgeable offers you advice, you must believe that she has good intentions. You must answer her with great kindness and, while being mindful of the truth, appear to agree with what she says, as much as possible (CSG 185).

~

If my words must always be clear and truthful, I must ensure that I am not suspicious of others. While respecting their good intentions, I will stay clear about and watchful of the truth. Those who try to deceive others are only deceiving themselves. Lord, help me to always be respectful.

"The harvest is plentiful, but the laborers are few; therefore ask the Lord of the harvest to send out laborers into his harvest" (Mt 9:37–38).

~

God made me understand that there are souls that his mercy does not tire of waiting for, to whom he gives his light by degrees. Also, I was careful not to move his time ahead, and I waited patiently until it pleases Jesus to make it come (Ms C, 21r).

~

If the workers do not hurry to the harvest, it's undoubtedly because your time is yet to come and that those called haven't been totally filled by your light. Lord, may everything go according to your heart and not our own ideas.

"And if anyone forces you to go one mile, go also the second mile. Give to everyone who begs from you, and do not refuse anyone who wants to borrow from you" (Mt 5:41–42).

~

At times, we must decline to do a favor because of our work. (...) There is such a gracious way to refuse what we cannot give so that the refusal is as pleasurable as the gift. It is true that we are less shy to ask a favor of a Sister who is always available; however Jesus said, "Do not avoid those who want to borrow from you" (Ms C, 18r).

~

There is a way to do a favor which is not charity, but kindness. There is a way to refuse to do a favor which isn't closing oneself to others but an expression of a true impossibility. The gift as well as the refusal should always be an expression of love. Lord, may I always be ready to help someone in need.

Eleventh Tuesday in Ordinary Time

"For if you love those who love you, what reward do you have?...And if you greet only your brothers and sisters, what more are you doing than others?" (Mt 5:46–47).

～

[The sister who displeased me said to me] "Would you tell me (…) what draws you to me? Each time you look at me, I see you smile." Oh, what attracted me was Jesus, hiding in the depth of her soul....Jesus who sweetens what is the most bitter....I answered her that I smiled because I was happy to see her [in a spiritual way] (Ms C, 14r).

～

How can I smile at someone who irritates and bothers me if not by seeing your presence deep inside of them, Lord? But to do this, I ask you to change my glance into your loving glance.

"Beware of practicing your piety before others in order to be seen by them; for then you have no reward from your Father in heaven" (Mt 6:1).

~

I was the donkey who, having seen the caresses given to the little dog, went and put his heavy paw on the table to receive his share. But, alas, even if I did not receive a whipping like that poor animal, I did receive my just return. This cured me for life of the desire to attract attention (Ms A, 42r).

~

Along the way, one may be tempted to attract attention to oneself to get noticed, to get a promotion, to gain power or to impress others. It is far better to draw the attention of God's tender and loving glance to us to help us live according to his will. Lord, help me resist temptations.

"Pray then in this way: Our Father in heaven, hallowed be your name. Your kingdom come…" (Mt 6:9–10).

∿

The little bird would like to fly toward that brilliant Sun which enchants its eyes. It would like to imitate its brothers, the eagles, who it sees soaring all the way to the divine home of the Blessed Trinity….Alas, all it can do is lift up its wings, but to soar, that is not within its power (Ms B, 5r).

∿

How can my fragile soul soar to your house of love, to the peak of love, if not by letting myself be carried by the Divine Eagle, your Beloved Son, the brilliant Sun of Glory? With him and through him, I could call you by your name: Father. Lord, help my fragile soul soar to your great heights.

"The eye is the lamp of the body. So, if your eye is healthy, your whole body will be full of light" (Mt 6:22).

∼

As long as you want it, my Beloved, your little bird will remain weak and without wings, all the while keeping its eyes fixed upon you. It wants to be mesmerized by your divine glance, it wants to fall prey to your love" (Ms B, 5v).

∼

How can my eye be the lamp of the body if I don't let your luminous glance draw me to you, Jesus, and if I don't keep my eyes fixed upon you? Then, all darkness will vanish and I will be illuminated by you, my heart opened to your transforming love. Lord, let your light shine into my heart.

"Therefore I tell you, do not worry about your life, what you will eat or what you will drink, or about your body, what you will wear. Is not life more than food, and the body more than clothing?" (Mt 6:25).

~

You are so worried about the future, as if it was you who must arrange it. I understand your concern. You are always saying to yourself: Oh Lord, what will happen tomorrow? Everyone looks for omens like this, that's the common way. Only the poor in spirit do not seek them (CSG 30).

~

It's one thing to worry about tomorrow at the risk of living removed from the present. It's another to take care of the future while being true to today. By putting my life in your hands, Lord, I rest in peace, knowing you open the future to me through you. Keep me at peace.

"Do not fear those who kill the body but cannot kill the soul; rather fear him who can destroy both soul and body in hell" (Mt 10:28).

～

The little bird is not afraid of the vultures, the reflections of the demons. It is not destined to be their prey, but that of the eagle, which it gazes upon at the center of the Sun of love (Ms B, 5v).

～

When you light our way, your light penetrates our lives. There is no fear of eternal death. You are the Lord of life. You want me in your love forever. Lord, light my love.

Twelfth Monday in Ordinary Time

"Why do you see the speck in your neighbor's eye, but do not notice the log in your own eye?" (Mt 7:3).

~

When the devil tries to show my soul the flaws of another Sister (...) I rush to find her virtues. I tell myself that if I saw her fall once, she could very well have won many victories. (...) And what could appear to be a mistake could be an act of virtue by its intention (Ms C, 12v–13r).

~

True charity makes us look for qualities and good will, not faults and mistakes in others. Perhaps I need to change the way I look at others to truly love them, and the way I look at myself to be clearheaded and wise. Lord, help me change.

Twelfth Tuesday in Ordinary Time

"Do not give what is holy to dogs; and do not throw your pearls before swine..." (Mt 7:6).

~

Only charity could expand my heart. Oh Jesus, ever since this gentle flame began to consume it [my heart], I happily follow your new commandment....I want to follow it until the blessed day when, in uniting myself with the virginal cortège, I will be able to follow you into infinite spaces, singing your new hymn of love (Ms C, 16r).

~

I must keep what is sacred as such. Through it, my daily life is sprinkled with the Divine. The sacred pearl is you, Jesus, the beloved, whose love lights up my life and enables my heart to love you and sing of you. Lord, let me keep you as my holy pearl.

"Beware of false prophets....You will know them by their fruits" (Mt 7:15–16).

～

Vanity slips so easily into the heart!...A lady would say I have lovely hair....Someone else...would ask who was that pretty young girl. Those words, even more flattering because they weren't said in front of me, left an impression of joy on my soul. This clearly showed me how much I was filled with egotism (Ms A, 40r).

～

We encounter many flatterers on the road who sow the seeds of vanity and pride in the heart. False prophets are the sources of pleasure which deposit the seeds of egotism in others. I know that I have received what I am from you, Lord, but for your glory, not my own. Lord, protect me from my ego.

"The rain fell, the floods came, and the winds blew and beat on that house, but it did not fall, because it had been founded on rock" (Mt 7:25).

~

If the Dear Lord hadn't lavished his beneficial rays on his little flower, it would never have been able to adapt to earth. It was still too weak to withstand the rain and storms. It needed heat, gentle dew, and spring breezes. It never lacked any of these blessings. Jesus made it find them, even under the snow of hardship (Ms A, 13v).

~

I will stand tall on the road of life if you, Lord, set up barriers in front of my turmoils, if you give strength to my shy faith, if you aerate my confined existence. Under the chill of hardships, you support me because you are my rock.

Twelfth Friday in Ordinary Time

"Lord, if you choose, you can make me clean."…"I do choose. Be made clean!" (Mt 8:2–3).

~

I was truly insufferable because I was much too sensitive. If I happened to involuntarily upset someone I liked, instead of getting the upper hand, so as not to cry, (…) I cried my eyes out. And when I began to console myself about it, I cried for having cried (Ms A, 44v).

~

Undue sensitivity can harm the good progress of life. If I do act in this manner, help me work to overcome it. From you, Lord, I seek purification to go from sensitivity to tenderness.

Twelfth Saturday in Ordinary Time

That evening they brought to him many who were possessed with demons; and he cast out the spirits with a word, and cured all who were sick. This was to fulfill what had been spoken through the prophet Isaiah, "He took our infirmities and bore our diseases" (Mt 8:16–17).

~

How Our Lord is good…in the way he adjusts hardships to the strength he gives us (Ms A, 21r).

~

You show yourself, Jesus, as a God of kindness, sharing humankind's suffering, carrying their faults on your shoulders. But, you appear to me, at times, to be so far away, deaf to my requests. I don't know how to discover your consoling presence and strength. Lord, help me find you.

Thirteenth Sunday in Ordinary Time

"Those who find their life will lose it, and those who lose their life for my sake will find it" (Mt 10:39).

~

Little lamb…I did not say to completely break away from other humans, to scorn their love, (…) but just the opposite: to use them as stairs. Because to move away from humans only serves to do one thing: to walk along and get lost on the pathways on earth….To rise up, one must place a foot on the steps of humans and be attached only to me….Do you understand, little Lamb?" (LT 190).

~

At first sight, all separations reveal a loss and bring about suffering. Time is necessary for it to seem to be a good tiding for a life in which great happiness appears. Lord, make me understand.

"Teacher, I will follow you wherever you go" (Mt 8:19).

~

The little flower, transplanted on the mountain at Carmel, had to bloom in the shadow of the cross. The tears and blood of Jesus became its dew, and its Sun was his Adorable Face, veiled with tears....Up until then, I hadn't probed the depth of the hidden treasures in the Holy Face (Ms A, 71r).

~

To follow you up the hill where your cross is planted is my plan for a life in you. You draw me to you by your glorious humanity. Sainted Face of Love, light of resurrection, reveal your hidden depth to me.

"Why are you afraid, you of little faith?" Then he got up and rebuked the winds and the sea; and there was a dead calm (Mt 8:26).

~

My soul was like a frail skiff, left without a helmsman on a stormy sea....I know Jesus was there, sleeping on my boat, but the night was so dark that it was impossible for me to see him. (...) It was night, the deep night of the soul....I felt alone. (...) The Lord seemed to have deserted me (Ms A, 51r).

~

It is a profound night that instills fear when the tumult inside of myself reduces you to silence, Lord. It is a profound night which generates fear when no ray of light can penetrate, when you are silent and you leave me alone. It may be night; nevertheless, I believe you are there.

Then the whole town [from the country of the Gadarenes] came out to meet Jesus; and when they saw him, they begged him to leave their neighborhood (Mt 8:34).

~

One evening, not knowing how to tell Jesus I loved him and how much I wanted him to be loved and glorified everywhere, I painfully thought that he could never receive a single act of love from hell. Then, I told our Lord that to please him, I would agree to see myself thrown there, so that he would be loved eternally in that place of blasphemy (Ms A, 52r).

~

What a wound to your heart it must be when souls come out, not to greet you, but to chase you away! It's a road of no return for the person who behaves in this manner. This is my prayer: that all humankind will receive you in love.

Thirteenth Thursday in Ordinary Time

"But so that you may know that the Son of Man has authority on earth to forgive sins"—he then said to the paralytic—"Stand up, take your bed and go to your home" (Mt 9:6).

~

God gave me his infinite mercy, and through it I gaze upon and adore the other divine perfections! Then, they all appear beaming with love; even justice appears to me to be cloaked with love....What sweet happiness to think that God is just! That is to say, he takes into account our weaknesses and he knows perfectly well the fragility of our nature (Ms A, 83v).

~

Because you are love, Lord, you are the God of forgiveness. Because you are justice, you are the God who weighs the value of each life. But because your justice is cloaked with love, my weaknesses and frailties are buried in your infinite mercy. Lord, help me to my feet.

As Jesus was walking along, he saw a man called Matthew sitting at the tax booth; and he said to him, "Follow me." And he got up and followed him (Mt 9:9).

～

Through my tears, I told him [my Father] of my desire to enter Carmel. Then his tears mingled with mine, but he didn't say a word to discourage me from my vocation. (...) He was soon convinced that my desire was that of God himself. And through his deep faith, he said that the Lord was doing him a great honor to ask him in such a way for his children (Ms A, 50r).

～

In the heart of certain people, you give birth to the deep desire to take your own road of love, all the way to the complete gift of oneself. In agreeing to begin, renewed each day, you will always deserve my gratitude in love and humbleness of faith. Lord, show me the way to serve you.

"Why do we and the Pharisees fast often, but your disciples do not fast?" (Mt 9:14).

~

If this soul is complacent in its nice thoughts and says the prayer of the Pharisees, it becomes like a person dying of hunger before a well-laden table, while all the guests were feasting off it, sometimes throwing an envious glance at the person who has so much (Ms C, 19v).

~

To not satisfy one's hunger when you set the table with your Word and your Bread, that is what happens to someone who doesn't understand you are there, Lord, the nourishment of life. Such a fast is harmful, unlike the purifying fast that opens us to life. Lord, let me eat at your table.

Fourteenth Sunday in Ordinary Time

"Take my yoke upon you, and learn from me; for I am gentle and humble in heart, and you will find rest for your souls" (Mt 11:29).

~

What a blessing, when in the morning we feel no courage, no strength to practice virtue. (...) Instead of wasting time gathering a few little sequins, we draw from our gems. What a benefit at the end of the day....It is true that at times, we resist for a few instants, building up our treasures, that is a difficult moment. We are tempted to leave it all there, but in an unnoticed act of love, all is restored; Jesus smiles (LT 65).

~

You invite me to take the yoke of love which requires that I forget my self and place my soul into your hands. You remind me that strength and courage come from you. I will find respite when my daily life becomes an act of love for you. Lord, give me a resting place for my soul.

"My daughter has just died; but come and lay your hand on her, and she will live." And Jesus got up and followed him, with his disciples (Mt 9:18–19).

~

Why would death scare me? I have acted only for God. (...) I don't need a day of celebration to die. The day of my death will be the biggest of all feast days for me (CSG 166).

~

The day of death, a day of supreme celebration for those who lived their earthly life in the faithfulness of love, because this is the way to enter the eternal day of glory, Lord. It is a day of pain and sadness for those who mourn. You knew corporal death, Jesus, with its multitude of sorrows before you rose from the dead. Lord, give me the courage to face my death.

Fourteenth Tuesday in Ordinary Time

A demoniac who was mute was brought to Jesus. And when the demon had been cast out, the one who had been mute spoke; and the crowds were amazed and said, "Never has anything like this been seen in Israel" (Mt 9:32–33).

~

On earth, there are people who know how to get an invitation, how to edge their way in everywhere....If we ask God for something he's not planning to give us, he is so powerful and rich, he will make it a point of honor not to refuse us and will grant it (CSG 48).

~

Because you are the One who gives when what we ask of you conforms to your will, like a troublesome person I dare to edge my way in, all the way to you. Tear me away from my silence which makes me a prisoner within myself. Lord, make my words an echo of your Word.

Fourteenth Wednesday in Ordinary Time

Then Jesus summoned his twelve disciples and gave them authority over unclean spirits, to cast them out, and to cure every disease and every sickness....These twelve [apostles] Jesus sent out (Mt 10:1–5).

~

You are in investments—you! There are many who practice this profession. That's the last thing I would do, I would be afraid not to earn enough. I do just the opposite, I put away as much as possible of what I do and deposit it into God's bank, without worrying if I get a return or not (CSG 31–32).

～

Jesus, I am your messenger in the Church; however, in that mission, neither "investments for profit" nor "self-valorization" bring fruit. Lord, help me be a servant and missionary of the Gospel, in humility and generosity.

Fourteenth Thursday in Ordinary Time

"As you go, proclaim the good news, 'The kingdom of heaven has come near'" (Mt 10:7).

～

As a small flame, weak and shaky, can spark a large fire, God uses who he wants to extend his kingdom....So, there's nothing to boast about when we're used as his instruments. The Lord needs no one (CSG 161).

～

I am a little flame in an ordinary life; yet, you want me as a herald for your kingdom to come, because a spark can inflame a heart searching for you, and everyday actions can testify to your love. Lord, use me as you see fit.

Fourteenth Friday in Ordinary Time

"Be wise as serpents and innocent as doves" (Mt 10:16).

~

"My little girl, it seems to me that you must have little to say to your superiors!"..."But Mother [Superior], why do you say that?"..."Because your soul is extremely simple, but even when you become perfect, you will be even more simple because the closer we come to God, the more simple we become" (Ms A, 70v).

~

You, Lord, are the simple and unified being. I am complex by nature and can only make myself simpler through you and by being stripped of my self. To be shrewd gives me a careful outlook, to be naive gives me a clear standpoint. Lord, draw me to you, who are the simplest of all.

Fourteenth Saturday in Ordinary Time

"So do not be afraid; you are of more value than many sparrows" (Mt 10:31).

~

Oh Jesus, what will you say in answer to all my foolishness?...Is there a soul even smaller and more powerless than mine?...Yet, because of my weakness, you were happy, Lord, to grant my little childish desires. And today, you want to grant other desires, bigger than the universe (Ms B, 3r).

~

Little sparrow, you are less than nothing, yet God has given you a place in the chorus of birds. I am a weak being; Lord, you put great desires in me which give me worth in you, so that I sing in the universe. Hear my song.

Fifteenth Sunday in Ordinary Time

"But blessed are your eyes, for they see, and your ears, for they hear" (Mt 13:16).

~

I have learned through experience that happiness only entails hiding oneself, remaining ignorant of creation. I understood that without love, all deeds are for nothing, even the most brilliant, like raising the dead or converting people (Ms A, 81v).

~

I only see you, Lord, through the invisibility of faith. I hear you only in the silence of my heart, because you are the hidden God who we discover, not in the thundering noise of the world, but in a silent heart-to-heart meeting with love. Lord, may I see and hear you.

Fifteenth Monday in Ordinary Time

"Whoever welcomes you welcomes me, and whoever welcomes me welcomes the one who sent me" (Mt 10:40).

~

My Lord, I want to know! What you would do to the little one who could answer your calling? I continued my search and this is what I found: "Like a mother caresses her child, this is how I will comfort you. I will carry you close to my breast and rock you on my lap" (Ms C, 3r).

~

The little child who can do nothing for himself leans on the adult who welcomes him. He feels safe in the arms of the one who loves him. Jesus, I welcome you into my soul and you open the sure way that leads to the Father. In him, we find all tenderness and security. Lord, show me the sure way.

"Woe to you, Chorazin! Woe to you, Bethsaida! For if the deeds of power done in you had been done in Tyre and Sidon, they would have repented long ago in sackcloth and ashes" (Mt 11:21).

～

Lord, your child asks your forgiveness for her brothers and sisters. She agrees to eat the bread of pain for as long as you like. She does not want to get up from the table, laden with bitterness, where the poor sinners eat, until your designated day (Ms C, 6r).

～

Lord, have compassion for this world which is sinking deeper into evil. Have mercy for your children who don't know how to do penance. May your liberating forgiveness vindicate sinners. I offer you all the bitterness of life so that the hardened hearts of sinners will melt upon meeting your love.

Fifteenth Wednesday in Ordinary Time

"No one knows the Son except the Father, and no one knows the Father except the Son and anyone to whom the Son chooses to reveal him" (Mt 11:27).

~

I searched all the holy books to find an indication of the elevator, the object of my desire. I read these words which came from the mouth of Eternal Wisdom: "If someone is VERY SMALL, *let him come to me." Then I came, discovering I had found what I was searching for (Ms C, 3r).*

~

Your knowledge of the Father, Lord Jesus, reveals your filial love for him, and, in your human form, you expressed the condition of being very small. Give me the intense desire to know the Father. Make it so that I intensively live my filial life by discovering him through you.

Fifteenth Thursday in Ordinary Time

"Take my yoke upon you, and learn from me...For my yoke is easy, and my burden is light" (Mt 11:29–30).

~

We are in an era of inventions. These days, one doesn't have to bother to climb stairs because the wealthy have

elevators to easily replace them. Me, I would like to find
an elevator to lift myself all the way up to Jesus, because
I am too small to climb the harsh staircase of perfection
(Ms C, 2v–3r).

∽

One climbs the road to perfection step by step, carrying
the yoke which joins me to you, Jesus, because the road of
a disciple is the same as the that of the Master. But [I know]
the strength of love linked with the power of your blessing
helps my ascension. Lord, let me share the yoke.

Fifteenth Friday in Ordinary Time

"I tell you, something greater than the temple is here. But
if you had known what this means, 'I desire mercy and not
sacrifice,' you would not have condemned the guiltless" (Mt
12:6–7).

∽

You know better than I of my weakness. (…) You know
very well that I could never have loved my Sisters as you
love them if you, Jesus, didn't love them again in me.
(…) You have made a new commandment. Oh how I
love it, since it gives me the assurance that your will is to
love in me all those you order me to love (Ms C, 12v).

∽

We are often too quick to condemn people based on what is said about them or their appearance, while you, Lord, always put your love and mercy first. Love in me all those I should love. May I love you in them.

Fifteenth Saturday in Ordinary Time

"Here is my servant, whom I have chosen, my beloved, with whom my soul is well pleased. I will put my Spirit upon him, and he will proclaim justice....He will not break a bruised reed or quench a smoldering wick until he brings justice to victory" (Mt 12:18, 20).

~

I wanted nothing but to love you. (...) Your love advised me from as early on as my childhood; it grew with me, and now it is an abyss so deep I can't measure its depth. Love attracts love, so, Jesus, my love throws itself toward you. It would like to fill the abyss that draws it but, alas, it is only a mere drop, lost in the ocean (Ms C, 34v–35r).

~

Lord, the sap of your love never stops making the reed that I am grow. Even when I am crushed, if the sap runs, I will be revived. I am certain of your love. Lord, make it so that my life will be that little drop of love which will make you happy.

"The one who sows the good seed is the Son of Man; the field is the world, and the good seed are the children of the kingdom; the weeds are the children of the evil one" (Mt 13:37–38).

~

Jesus likes to lavish his gifts on a few of his humans, but quite often it's to attract other hearts. Then, when he has reached his goal, he completely strips the souls which are the most precious to him. (…) It seems to them that they're no longer good for anything, (…) but Jesus creates the seed in them which must grow in heaven (LT 147).

~

To plant a seed [in soil] is an act of hope for a good harvest. Lord, you deposit your seed of life in me through your Eucharist, which will become eternal life only if my heart is fertile soil. May I not disappoint you.

Sixteenth Monday in Ordinary Time

"Teacher, we wish to see a sign from you" (Mt 12:38).

~

You don't feel your love for your HUSBAND; you would like your heart to be a flame that goes up towards him without the slightest smoke. Be careful that this smoke around you doesn't mask your view of your love for Jesus, and that the flame can only be seen by him. At least this way he has all of it, because as soon as he lets us get a little glance of it, self-love rushes in like a strong wind that blows out everything (LT 81).

~

If I should ask you for a sign of your love, would I still believe in your love? Neither the feeling nor the excitement will make me understand. I believe in your immense love which feeds my little flame. Lord, help my flame to endure.

Sixteenth Tuesday in Ordinary Time

"For whoever does the will of my Father in heaven is my brother and sister and mother" (Mt 12:50).

~

What it [my soul] may not know, perhaps, is the love that Jesus feels for it, a love that asks for it ALL. (...) He doesn't want to put a limit on the HOLINESS of his lily, his

own limit is that there is none!...Why would there be
any? We are bigger than the whole universe; one day, we
will have a divine existence ourselves (LT 83).

~

You are the one who wants to be first in each person's heart,
one who asks for all. How would I respond to your love if
not by carrying out the will of the Father, as you have done?
Then, I walk the road of holiness. Lord, renew my efforts.

Sixteenth Wednesday in Ordinary Time

"And as he sowed, some seeds fell on the path, and the
birds came and ate them up" (Mt 13:4).

~

FORGOTTEN!...Yes, I want to be forgotten, not just by hu-
mans, but also by myself. I would like to be so reduced to
nothing that I would have no desires [except]... the glory
of my Jesus, that's all. For my own glory, I give it up to him
and if he seems to forget me, oh well! He is free to do so
since I no longer belong to myself, but to him (LT 103).

~

I am a little seed among other seeds, chosen by your sower's
hand to be buried on earth. I give myself up to the warmth of
your love. I will be forgotten because it is the fruit that will
interest you, not the seed. I no longer belong to myself, but
to you. Lord, may the fruit of my love be your glory.

"To you it has been given to know the secrets of the king-dom of heaven" (Mt 13:11).

~

What is it then to ask to be enticed? (...) Here is my prayer: I ask Jesus to entice me into the flames of his love, to unite me so closely with him so that he lives and acts in me. I feel that the more the fire of love will ignite my heart, the more I will say "entice me," as well as the souls who will come close to me, (...) because a soul ignited by love cannot stay idle (Ms C, 35v–36r).

~

The more I grow in the knowledge you give me of your mystery, the more it entices me. I possess the mystery of life, thanks to the fire of your love. Lord, may I burn with this love so that my life, by its attraction to you, draws my brothers and sisters into the search for your mystery.

"What was sown on good soil, this is the one who hears the word and understands it" (Mt 13:23).

~

It is truly the "Divine Beggar of Love" who asks for hospitality and says "thank you" by always asking for more in proportion to what he receives. He feels that the hearts he speaks to understand that "the greatest honor God could give to a soul is not to give it a great deal but to ask a great deal from it" (LT 172).

~

The better the soil, the more hope the sower has for it. All that I am, I have received from you. But because you feed my soul with your word, I understand that you always expect more. The more you ask, the more you love, and the more hope you have for love. Lord, beg ever more love from me.

Sixteenth Saturday in Ordinary Time

"The kingdom of heaven may be compared to someone who sowed good seed in his field; but while everybody was asleep, an enemy came and sowed weeds among the wheat" (Mt 13:24–25).

～

I always see the good side of things. There are those who perceive things in a way that gives them the most sorrow. For me, it is the opposite. If I only have pure suffering, if the sky is so dark that I see no light, good! I draw my joy from it….I feast on it! (DE 35) (DE 27.5.6).

～

The enemy takes pleasure in planting all the traps along my route which slow my progress. The presence of weeds could even put me to sleep. Divine Sower, without being afraid of the bad side, make me see the good side of people and events instead, so that in this way the good grain of life will nourish my hope.

"On finding one pearl of great value, he went and sold all that he had and bought it" (Mt 13:46).

~

Jesus is a hidden treasure (...) which few souls know how to find because he is hidden and the world likes things that shine. (...) He doesn't want us to love him for his gifts; it is he who should be our reward. To find something hidden, one must also hide; our life should therefore be a mystery. We have to look like Jesus, whose face was hidden (LT 145).

~

Only an expert can estimate the value of a pearl. Only he who knows you, because he is close to you, becomes able to appreciate the gift of yourself. Jesus, my hidden treasure, arrange so that I will always search for you.

"[The mustard] is the smallest of all the seeds, but when it has grown it is the greatest of shrubs and becomes a tree, so that the birds of the air come and make nests in its branches" (Mt 13:32).

~

It seems that I never looked for anything but the truth. Yes, I understood the humility of the heart....It seems that I am humble. All that I ever wrote about was my desire for suffering. Oh, even so, it is true. And I do not regret having given myself to love (DE 185) (DE 30.9).

~

Garden shrubs are not trees of the forest. If you gave me the gift to grow, I will stay true to myself and keep my humility of heart. As I am a little seed, I could only hope to be a shrub. Lord, help me grow and remain humble.

"The one who sows the good seed is the Son of Man; the field is the world, and the good seed are the children of the kingdom" (Mt 13:37–38).

~

I am always happy with what God asks of me. I don't worry about what God asks of others, and I don't think I am more worthy because he asks even more from me. What pleases me, what I would choose—if I had the chance—is exactly what God wants of me. I am always happy with my share (CSG 60).

~

I am your seed thrown into this world here, a seed from which you hope to produce choice fruit. Admittedly, your demands are great, but they concur with my deep calling. Lord, I want what you want. I am linked to you.

"The kingdom of heaven is like treasure hidden in a field, which someone found and hid; then in his joy he goes and sells all that he has and buys that field" (Mt 13:44).

~

Yes, life is a treasure....Each moment is (...) an eternity seeing God face to face, being one with him. There is only Jesus, there's no one else....Therefore, let us love him madly and save souls for him. (...) We are so little...and yet Jesus only wants the salvation of all souls to depend upon our sacrifices, our love. He begs us for souls....Oh, let us understand the meaning of his glance (LT 96).

~

Jesus, you are my sole treasure, the object of my soul's deep contemplation, whom I like to reveal to whoever searches for the true values in life. Jesus, you are my whole life. Make my love so strong that it will bring those searching for the kingdom to you.

"Again, the kingdom of heaven is like a net that was thrown into the sea and caught fish of every kind" (Mt 13:47).

~

The riches of heaven are loaned to me by God who could take them back and I would have no right to complain. However, the riches which come directly from God, the surge of intelligence and of the heart, deep thoughts, all of that forms a wealth one becomes attached to, like his own, which no one has the right to touch (Ms C, 18v–19r).

~

In the swarming waters of my life, the fishing net reminds me of your many gifts that dwell within me, like the awakening of my spirit, the love of my heart, the thirst for knowledge. May you be blessed, Lord, for this richness of life which makes up my worth.

He came to his hometown and began to teach the people in their synagogue, so that they were astounded and said, "Where did this man get this wisdom and these deeds of power?" (Mt 13:54).

~

I learned a great deal by fulfilling the mission you have given me [with the novices]. Above all, I was forced to practice what I taught others. So now, I can say it, Jesus gave me the blessing of not being more attached to the riches of the spirit and heart than to those of earth (Ms C, 19r).

~

Divine Wisdom, Jesus, by speaking, you reveal yourself, for you live and say what you are. In this way, I learn from you that my being is the foundation of my word, and my word is received only if my behavior clarifies it. Lord, make me practice what you have taught me.

Seventeenth Saturday in Ordinary Time

For Herod had arrested John, bound him, and put him in prison on account of Herodias, his brother Philip's wife, because John had been telling him, "It is not lawful for you to have her" (Mt 14:3–4).

～

Even if I had all the sins that could be committed on my conscience, I would go with my heart broken with regrets and throw myself into the arms of Jesus, because I know how he cherishes the prodigal child who comes back to him. It is not because God, in his kind mercy, kept my soul from mortal sin, that I rise to him in trust and love (Ms C, 36v–37r).

～

The sin of separation can injure a human heart. Even if it severely breaks your paternal heart, you don't stop at that to await the return of your child to shower him with your love. Lord, knowing the meaning of sin, help me believe in love.

Taking the five loaves and the two fish, he looked up to heaven, and blessed and broke the loaves, and gave them to the disciples, and the disciples gave them to the crowds (Mt 14:19).

~

It was a true exchange of love: I gave the blood of Jesus to the souls and I offered these same souls back, refreshed by his divine dew. In this way, I felt I was quenching his thirst, and the more I gave him to drink, the greater the thirst of my poor little soul grew. He gave me this passionate thirst for the most delicious beverage of his love (Ms A, 46v).

~

You always wait for my humble gift to fulfill your exchange of love with me. It is then that your own gift draws mine into undreamt-of depths which reveal your satisfied, yet always demanding, love. The fact that I always thirst for you shows your loving presence.

Now when Jesus heard this [about the death of John the Baptist], he withdrew from there in a boat to a deserted place by himself (Mt 14:13).

~

The trials of Jesus, what a mystery! Yes he had some, and he is often all alone to press the grapes for wine. He searches for people to console him, but can find none.... Many are there to serve Jesus when they need him for their consolation, but few agree to keep Jesus company, sleeping on the waves or suffering in the garden of agony. Who will serve Jesus for himself? Ah, that will be us (LT 165).

~

One normally handles the severe trials of life in solitude because it is too difficult to share with others at those times. Jesus, your solitude at the death of John the Baptist and at your own agony is a mystery to us. Lord, give me the grace to enter into the mystery of your redemptive suffering.

Eighteenth Tuesday in Ordinary Time

But by this time the boat, battered by the waves, was far from the land, for the wind was against them. And early in the morning he came walking toward them on the sea. But when the disciples saw him walking on the sea, they were terrified....Peter answered him, "Lord, if it is you, command me to come to you on the water." He said, "Come" (Mt 14:24–29).

~

Sometimes (...) the little bird's heart finds itself bombarded by the storm. It seems to believe that nothing exists except the clouds surrounding it. That is the moment of perfect joy for the poor little weak creature. What happiness for it to stay there all the same to try to find the invisible light which hides from its faith (Ms B, 5r).

~

What do I do when I am tossed around on the road of life, when fear overcomes me because my defenses crumble? I must search for you, hidden light, until my faith finds you and helps me hear your reassuring word: "Come."

"Even the dogs eat the crumbs that fall from their masters' table." Then Jesus answered her, "Woman, great is your faith!" (Mt 15:27–28).

~

How sweet it is for me to look at you and then fulfill the Lord's will! Ever since he allowed me to suffer temptations against faith, he has greatly increased the spirit of faith in my heart. This makes me see in you, not only a Mother who loves me and whom I love, but, above all, one who makes me see Jesus living in your soul and telling me his will through you (Ms C, 11r).

~

The little dog prefers something other than crumbs, but they satisfy, in part, his hunger. I would prefer a faith, simple and strong, over a faith shaken with temptations. But if I only get the crumbs of faith from your table, oh my Master, they will strengthen my spirit of faith. Lord, nourish my faith.

Eighteenth Thursday in Ordinary Time

"Blessed are you, Simon son of Jonah! For flesh and blood has not revealed this to you, but my Father in heaven" (Mt 16:17).

∽

Charity gave me the key to my vocation. I understood that if the Church had a body, (…) it had a heart and this heart was burning with love. (…) Yes, I found my place in the Church and this place, Lord, you have given to me….In the heart of the Church, my Mother, I will be love….In this way, I will be everything (Ms B, 3v).

∽

Happy are those who welcome the presence of Trinitarian love into their life. Happy are those who see the gift of their own love in the Body of Christ. Happy are those who hold their place in the Church as a witness to love. Lord, may I always be happy in you.

Eighteenth Friday in Ordinary Time

"If any want to become my followers, let them deny themselves and take up their cross and follow me" (Mt 16:24).

∽

Suffering became appealing to me. It had charms which delighted me without me even knowing them. Up until then I suffered without loving the suffering, but since that day, I felt a true love for it (Ms A, 36r–v).

~

The cross will always have a very strong bitter taste. If you carried it, Lord Jesus, it is with the strength you drew from the love for the Father and for us. I am not certain that suffering appeals to me. Lord, when it happens, help me give it a meaning of love to live through it.

Eighteenth Saturday in Ordinary Time

"If you have faith the size of a mustard seed, you will say to this mountain, 'Move from here to there,' and it will move; and nothing will be impossible for you" (Mt 17:20).

~

My heart was broken when I went to midnight Mass [in 1887]. I was really counting on attending Mass behind the gates of Carmel. This was such a great trial for my faith, but [Jesus] made me understand that to those whose faith is equal to a mustard seed (…) he gives the power to move mountains, so as to strengthen this little faith. But he won't perform any miracles for his close friends before having first tested their faith (Ms A, 67v).

~

Sometimes I create mountains by confusing my faith with the conditions and circumstances where it finds itself. That may be destructive. Lord, keep this first little seed of faith, which is often forced to grow in the midst of obstacles, alive in me.

Nineteenth Sunday in Ordinary Time

And after he [Jesus] had dismissed the crowds, he went up the mountain by himself to pray (Mt 14:23).

~

I should be upset with myself for falling asleep [for the past seven years] during my prayers and acts of thanksgiving. Oh well, I am not upset....I think that children give as much pleasure to their parents when they sleep as when they are awake. (…) Finally, I think that "the Lord sees our weakness and remembers that we are only dust" (Ms A, 75r–76v).

~

Jesus, I feel the intensity of your prayer. I am far from being like you. I am often somewhere else or asleep. You know my weakness and sometimes my lack of preparation for prayer. I am here before you, like a small child, awake or asleep, with my heart full of love for you. Lord, help me overcome my weakness.

"From whom do kings of the earth take toll or tribute? From their children or from others?"...Peter said, "From others." Jesus said to him, "Then the children are free" (Mt 17:25–27).

～

There are no obstacles for children; they get through everywhere. The big souls can overcome things, toss aside the difficulties, and reach a way to rise above it all by reasoning or virtue. But we who are so small must not try that. (…) To give in to things is to not look at them too closely, not to reason them out (CSG 44).

～

The ability to rise above things is given to the big souls, who are capable of knowledgeable thinking. To give in to things is for the little souls, who throw themselves into your love, without a word and find themselves further along, beyond the obstacles.

Nineteenth Tuesday in Ordinary Time

"Whoever becomes humble like this child is the greatest in the kingdom of heaven" (Mt 18: 4).

～

Children do not work to make a place for themselves. If they are good, it is to please their parents. So, we must not work to become saints, but work to please God (CSG 46).

～

To work to make oneself noticed is not love for others but self-love, while to please someone is proof of the freely given love one has for that person. Lord, what matters the most in my day-to-day life is to please you, out of love, by the giving of myself, without any ulterior motives, just like a child.

Nineteenth Wednesday in Ordinary Time

"If another member of the church sins against you, go and point out the fault when the two of you are alone. If the member listens to you, you have regained that one" (Mt 18:15).

～

We should be very happy that our neighbor denigrated us at times, because if no one did so, what would we become? It is to our advantage (CSG 18).

～

To be showered with praise is more pleasant than to be denigrated, but it is to no advantage. It is better if someone justly tells me what they think of me or what they blame me for, so they can help me change. Happy are those who find a brother or sister along the road who will enlighten them and set them straight. Lord, help me accept criticism lovingly so I can use it to change.

Nineteenth Thursday in Ordinary Time

"Lord, if another member of the church sins against me, how often should I forgive? As many as seven times?" (Mt 18:21).

~

To believe oneself imperfect and find others perfect, that is happiness. If someone recognizes you to be without virtue, that doesn't take anything away from you, it doesn't make you poorer. It's they who lose their inner joy, because there's nothing nicer than thinking well of your neighbor (CSG 25).

~

Lord, forgiveness always flows from your love, but I can't give it to anyone unless I receive it first from you. If I always consider myself poor and imperfect and learn to always see the good in my neighbor, I will know happiness. Lord, enlighten me and teach me forgiveness.

"There are others who have given up the possibility of marriage for the sake of the kingdom of heaven. He who can accept this, should accept it" (Mt 19:12).

~

In religious life, (…) by giving oneself to God, the heart doesn't lose its natural tenderness. To the contrary, this tenderness grows by becoming purer and more divine. Beloved Mother, I love you and my Sisters with this kind of tenderness. I am happy to fight for the good of this family (Ms C, 9r).

~

By dedicating ourselves to God through celibacy, we don't build a heart of stone. Our love, given totally to Christ and fulfilled by him, keeps us in this tenderness of heart, beyond sentimentality. Moreover, true love requires deprivation, doesn't it?

Then little children were being brought to him in order that he might lay his hands on them and pray....And he laid his hands on them and went on his way (Mt 19:13–15).

～

Oh Mother! I am too small to speak beautiful words to make you believe that I have a great deal of humility. I prefer to simply admit that the All-Powerful did great things in the soul of the child of his divine Mother. The biggest of these is to have shown her smallness, her powerlessness to her (Ms C, 4r).

～

The more I come before you in the truth of my smallness and powerlessness, the more your heart is touched and the more your hand touches me to lead me down the road of life where I shall accomplish great feats, which will be your work in me. Lord, I am truly small; guide me.

Twentieth Sunday in Ordinary Time

"Woman, great is your faith! Let it be done for you as you wish" (Mt 15:28).

～

May all those who are not enlightened with the bright torch of faith, see it finally shine....Oh Jesus, if it is necessary for the table that was soiled by them to be purified by a soul you love, I would be willing to eat the bread of hardship there alone until it would please you to let me enter your brilliant kingdom (Ms C, 6r).

～

Faith is always a subdued light. The more it is alive in me, the more it will show in my daily life, and the more I will be a guiding light to you. But humankind has the freedom to accept or reject faith. Lord, help my light guide them all to you.

Twentieth Monday in Ordinary Time

"Why do you ask me about what is good? There is only one who is good" (Mt 19:17).

～

Oh my Lord, (...) will it only be your justice that will receive the sacrificed souls?...Doesn't your merciful love need them too?....Everywhere, it is misunderstood, rejected. The hearts to which you want to give your love turn to humans, asking them for happiness with their miserable affection, instead of (...) accepting your infinite love (Ms A, 84r).

~

If I find it difficult to be misunderstood when I show someone some kindness, how you must suffer, God of plenty, if I misunderstand your merciful love, or even worse, if I reject it. Lord, give me a loving and understanding heart.

Twentieth Tuesday in Ordinary Time

"Truly I tell you, it will be hard for a rich person to enter the kingdom of heaven" (Mt 19:23).

~

If our Lord wants nice thoughts and sublime feelings, he has his angels....He could even have created souls so perfect that they would not have had our kind of weaknesses. But no, he delights in poor, miserable, and weak humans....Without a doubt, this pleases him more (CSG 29).

~

Flashiness, knowledge, prestige, and social standing are many forms of wealth which appeal to humankind. Jesus, you who made yourself poor, are attracted to the small, the weak, and the sinners. You save them and lift them up with your love. Which path am I really on? Lord, show me the right way.

"The kingdom of heaven is like a landowner who went out early in the morning to hire laborers for his vineyard. After agreeing with the laborers for the usual daily wage, he sent them into his vineyard....He went out about nine o'clock,... about noon,...about three o'clock, and...about five o'clock... and said to them, 'You also go into the vineyard'" (Mt 20:1ff).

~

Jesus, if I would like to write down all my desires, I would have to borrow your book of life. Recorded there are the deeds of all the saints. These are the things I would like to have accomplished for you (Ms B, 3r).

~

If I am happy for those who were hired at five o'clock, I give thanks for having been called in the early morning to work for and with you. Without a doubt, I could have been even more generous. Lord, keep me passionate in my desire to serve you to the very end.

"The kingdom of heaven may be compared to a king who gave a wedding banquet for his son."..."Look, I have prepared my dinner, my oxen and my fat calves have been slaughtered, and everything is ready; come to the wedding banquet" (Mt 22:2–4).

～

You also know that Jesus gave me more than one bitter chalice, which he removed from my lips before I drank from them, but not before having made me enjoy their bitterness (Ms C, 8v).

～

Before taking part in the wedding feast of your Son in your kingdom, I must drink from the cup of life with its bitter taste or inhale its pungent odor. Because the call to come to you is so strong, it helps me go beyond the present and conquer my misgivings. Lord, may I always hear your call and go beyond the present.

Twentieth Friday in Ordinary Time

"Teacher, which commandment in the law is the greatest?" Jesus said to him, "You shall love the Lord your God with all your heart, and with all your soul, and with all your mind."... "You shall love your neighbor as yourself" (Mt 22:36–37, 39).

～

The rule of love followed the rule of fear, and love chose me as its sacrificial victim; me, a weak and imperfect human....Yes, for love to be completely satisfied, it must lower itself all the way to nothingness and change that nothingness into fire (Ms B, 3v).

～

All love assumes that we forget ourselves and sacrifice ourselves for the other person. When lived with respect and consideration, it takes us to a type of humility. In humility, like you, Jesus, on the cross, my love becomes a burning fire when it comes in contact with your love. Lord, accept my love.

Twentieth Saturday in Ordinary Time

"The scribes and Pharisees sit on Moses' seat; therefore, do whatever they teach you and follow it; but do not do as they do, for they do not practice what they teach" (Mt 23:2–3).

～

I always wanted to be a saint. (...) Instead of being discouraged, I told myself: the Lord would not inspire unachievable desires. Therefore, I can aspire to sainthood in spite of my smallness (Ms C, 2v).

More from witnesses than from preachers, witnesses to holiness whose life is a faithful reflection of the Gospel as shown by their words and deeds. I feel this desire deep inside me. Lord, I ask your blessing to help me accomplish it.

Twenty-First Sunday in Ordinary Time

"But who do you say that I am?" Simon Peter answered, "You are the Messiah, the Son of the living God" (Mt 16:15–16).

I don't depreciate the deep thoughts which nourish the soul and unite it to God, but for a long time I understood that one must not rely upon them and perceive perfection as consisting of receiving many lights. The nicest thoughts are nothing without deeds (Ms C, 19v).

The enlightenment about who you are, Jesus, comes to me from heaven. The more it penetrates me, the more it pushes me to act as your messenger. Lord, make sure there is always a vital connection between my faith and deeds.

Twenty-First Monday in Ordinary Time

"Woe to you, scribes and Pharisees, hypocrites!...Woe to you, blind guides" (Mt 23:15–16).

~

It is a great trial to see everything black, but this doesn't completely depend upon you; do what you can, (...) then be assured that Jesus will do the rest. He will not let you fall into the dreaded quagmire....Console yourself. (...) In heaven you will no longer see everything as black, but all in white....Yes, everything will be dressed in the divine whiteness of our Spouse (LT 241).

~

It is always harmful to deceive ourselves or to show ourselves to be something we are not, as it is a lack of hope to see all situations black. It is better to let your shining whiteness restore me and establish me in the truth. Lord, light up the blackness in my life.

Twenty-First Tuesday in Ordinary Time

"You have neglected the weightier matters of the law: justice and mercy and faith" (Mt 23:23).

~

I am a very small soul who can offer God only little things. All too often I forget some of these little sacrifices which give so much peace to the soul. This doesn't discourage me. I accept having a little less peace and work to be more vigilant at another time (Ms C, 31r).

~

Even if you ask me to fulfill the important parts of your law of love, I can't presume to offer you big things. I am not discouraged by this. Lord, with your blessings, I will faithfully proceed to you with a heightened vigilance.

Twenty-First Wednesday in Ordinary Time

"So you [scribes and Pharisees] also on the outside look righteous to others, but inside you are full of hypocrisy and lawlessness" (Mt 23:28).

~

I feel I must make myself small to certain souls, and not be afraid to humiliate myself by admitting my conflicts and defeats. Seeing that I have the same weaknesses, my Sisters also admit their faults to me and rejoice that I understand them through experience (Ms C, 23v).

~

To appear to be what I am makes me be true to myself and makes me humble. In this way, I will be better able to understand others and be of help to them. Lord, keep me away from false appearances.

Twenty-First Thursday in Ordinary Time

"Blessed is that slave whom his master will find at work when he arrives" (Mt 24:46).

~

Céline, (...) perhaps you are going to believe that I always do what I say, but no! I am not always faithful, but I never get discouraged; I give myself up to Jesus' arms (LT 143).

~

My faithfulness is built, day by day, when I say yes to you with confidence. Jesus, extend your arms to me in my times of weakness so that I remain at work, or return to it.

Twenty-First Friday in Ordinary Time

"But at midnight there was a shout, 'Look! Here is the bridegroom! Come out to meet him'" (Mt 25:6).

~

Our Beloved was crazy to come to earth to search for sinners, to make them his friends, his intimate friends, his fellows—he who was perfectly happy with the two wonderful persons of the Trinity! We could never do for him what he did for us, and our actions, (...) which are only very reasonable actions, are much less than what our love would like to do (LT 169).

~

For me to become your brother, for me to share your intimacy and make me worthy of the nuptials, Jesus, the Beloved, you come to meet me. The vision of your love comes to me in the middle of the night and attracts me, so that, by going outside of myself, I will be everything to you. Lord, make me part of your love.

Twenty-First Saturday in Ordinary Time

"For to all those who have, more will be given, and they will have an abundance" (Mt 25:29).

⌣

Sole happiness on earth is for us to concentrate on always finding what Jesus gives us to be delicious. (…) If you want to be a saint, that will be easy, since you feel [from the bottom of your heart] that the world is nothing to you. You can therefore, like us, concentrate on "the only necessary thing," which means that while you are devoting yourself to exterior deeds, your only goal is this: to make Jesus happy, to unite yourself intimately with him (LT 257).

⌣

How could I not be in a state of abundance when you give yourself to me, Jesus? You are everything to me. Wherever I live or work, I will be fulfilled by bringing you joy and discovering you in my heart. Lord, may you dwell in me forever.

Twenty-Second Sunday in Ordinary Time

"But when you are invited, go and sit down at the lowest place....For all who exalt themselves will be humbled, and those who humble themselves will be exalted" (Lk 14:10–11).

∽

We must never search for what seems big in human eyes. (…) The only thing that is not envied is the lowest place; thus, it is the only place that is not vanity or an affliction of the soul....However, "the choice of man's way is not within his power," and sometimes we find ourselves wanting those things that shine. (…) Let us consider ourselves to be little souls that God must constantly support (LT 243).

∽

Shiny, showy things surely have more appeal than the lowest place, but it's deceptive. Lord, free me from vanity and pride. Support me in my humanity. I prefer productive discretion more than noisy notoriety.

All spoke well of him and were amazed at the gracious words that came from his mouth (Lk 4:22).

～

God is wonderful, but above all, he is lovable, so let us love him....Let us love him enough to suffer all that he asks us to, in his name, even the sorrows of the soul, thanklessness, anguish, apparent coldness....Oh, that is great love: to love Jesus without feeling the gentleness of that love....That is a martyr (LT 9).

～

Lord Jesus, your words, like your actions, always astonish me so much that I discover your kindness and love in them. It is another matter when I look inside myself and don't find them. That is a painful situation; however it allows me to say that I love you. Lord, ease my pain.

Twenty-Second Tuesday in Ordinary Time

They were astounded at his teaching, because he spoke with authority....And a report about him began to reach every place in the region (Lk 4:32–37).

~

My dear Céline, thank Jesus. He fills you with his choicest blessings if you always remain faithful by pleasing him in the little things and will find himself obliged to help you with the big ones. (...) That is the nature of Jesus. He gives through God but he wants the humility of the heart (LT 161).

~

Jesus, I am weak when it comes to understanding your mystery, but you are my teacher. May you be blessed for nourishing me with your word each day. May it be my light and my strength. Lord, let me do great things for you with humility.

Twenty-Second Wednesday in Ordinary Time

[Jesus] departed and went into a deserted place. And the crowds were looking for him; and when they reached him, they wanted to prevent him from leaving them (Lk 4:42).

~

Jesus, what use will my flowers and songs be to you? (...) These fragile and worthless petals, these songs of love from the smallest of hearts, will charm you; yes, these little nothings will please you (Ms B, 4v).

~

You welcomed this crowd which held you back, Lord Jesus. You read their thirst for love in their hearts, this desire to know you, this need to be freed. You heard the cries of the little ones. All of this made you happy. When I come out of my own deserts, Lord, help me be, like you, open to others?

Twenty-Second Thursday in Ordinary Time

[Jesus said,] "Put out into the deep water and let down your nets for a catch."…"Do not be afraid" (Lk 5:4–10).

~

He was even more merciful to me than he was to his disciples. Jesus himself took the net, threw it into the water and pulled it out, filled with fish….He made me a fisherman of souls, I felt a great desire to work at converting sinners. (…) In a word, I felt charity enter my heart, the need for me to forget myself to please him and since then, I have been happy (Ms A, 45v).

~

What a noble mission to be a fisherman of souls! But what patience and respect for others it requires! Lord, I must let your tenderness in so I can throw the net with charity, forgetting myself, because only you alone will bring in the net.

Twenty-Second Friday in Ordinary Time

"And no one after drinking old wine desires new wine, but says, 'The old is good'" (Lk 5:39).

～

I assure you that the Lord is much better than you believe. He is happy with just a glance, a sigh of love…. For me, I find perfection very easy to practice because I understood that all I had to do was to take Jesus by the heart. (…) Let us know, then, this prisoner, this God who becomes a beggar for our love (LT 191).

～

The truth of love is in its duration and refinement. Like wine, aging improves it. Lord, faithful to your love, may my own love find value and longevity.

Twenty-Second Saturday in Ordinary Time

"One sabbath while Jesus was going through the grain-fields, his disciples plucked some heads of grain, rubbed them in their hands, and ate them" (Lk 6:1).

～

I no longer feel it necessary to refuse all solace for my heart because my soul is strengthened by the only one I wanted to love. I happily see that by loving him, the

heart grows, that it can give incomparably more tender-
ness to those who are dear to it than if it had concen-
trated on selfish and fruitless love (Ms C, 22r).

~

Whoever has a heart enriched by Him who is love can perform acts that cannot be understood by those for whom
the letter of the law counts more than the spirit or by those
who cautiously withdraw within themselves. Lord, give me
a free and generous heart and an enlightened spirit.

Twenty-Third Sunday in Ordinary Time

"None of you can become my disciple if you do not give
up all your possessions" (Lk 14:33).

~

I did not expect to come to Carmel to receive praise; also
after the parlor visit [the interview], I never stopped
telling God that it was for him alone that I wanted to be
a Carmelite (Ms A, 26v).

~

Master, if you went to the extreme limits of self-depriva-
tion on the cross, I, your disciple, must free myself from
my sense of self. Then, you will be everything to me so that
I will act for you alone in my daily life. Lord, help me free
myself.

There was a man there whose right hand was withered (Lk 6:6).

~

Don't believe that I swim in consolation. Oh no, my solace is to have none on earth! Jesus, without showing me, or even making me hear his voice, teaches me in secret, not by using books (...) but, at times, guidance comes to me at the end of a prayer, like this one: "Here, I give you the teacher. He will teach you all you must do. I want to make you read from the book of life which contains all the knowledge about love" (LT 196).

~

No life exists without obstacles, and these handicaps affect me. You bring me solace along this road of life I take where your love is present but hidden. Isn't knowledge about love acquired from day to day? Lord, share this knowledge with me.

Twenty-Third Tuesday in Ordinary Time

And when day came, he called his disciples and chose twelve of them, whom he named apostles (Lk 6:13).

～

I read [in 1 Corinthians, chapters 12 and 13] (...) that not everyone can be apostles, prophets, doctors, and so on, and that the Church is made up of many different members and that an eye cannot be a hand....The answer was clear but it didn't fulfill my desires and didn't give me peace. (...) Without being discouraged, I continued reading and this phrase soothed me: 'Strive for the greater gifts and I will show you a still more excellent way.' (...) The greater gifts are none other than love....Charity is the still more excellent way that surely leads to God (Ms B, 3r–v).

～

One is called an apostle to allow oneself to be conquered by the love of Christ. Then, deeply filled with his love, we become witnesses. Lord, fill me with your love.

"Blessed are you....But woe to you when all speak well of you, for that is what their ancestors did to the false prophets" (Lk 6:20–24).

～

The knowledge of love, oh yes, these words echo gently in my soul. I want nothing more than this knowledge for my soul. Having given up all my wealth, like the wife in the sacred canticles, I feel that I have given nothing....I understand completely that only love can make us acceptable to God. I strive only for that love (LT 196).

～

Happy are those who learn through contact with the God of love that to love is to give, not to know. Unhappy are those who aren't open to the knowledge of love because they lose the only true possession. Happy are those who come to God with their entire capacity to love and receive our Lord unto themselves. Lord, I want to be one of those who are happy.

"Do not judge, and you will not be judged; do not condemn, and you will not be condemned. Forgive, and you will be forgiven" (Lk 6:37).

~

That also prevents me from having vanity when I am complimented because I tell myself: Since some take my little acts of virtue as imperfections, one could also mistakenly take for virtue what is an imperfection. (…) Only the Lord judges me. Also, (…) so as not to be judged at all, I always want to have charitable thoughts because Jesus said: "Do not judge, and you will not be judged" (Ms C, 13r–v).

~

It is presumptuous to want to judge the value of someone by relying solely upon what we see! Make me always have a charitable outlook and thoughts toward others. Father, you alone are the judge as you alone know what is in our hearts.

"A disciple is not above the teacher, but everyone who is fully qualified will be like the teacher" (Lk 6:40).

~

A soul isn't holy just because God uses it as an instrument. It is like an artist who uses this brush or that one. Why choose this one, or leave the other aside? It isn't any less a brush, and it could even be better than the other one. Anyway, to be used for the Master's work doesn't make one better. (…) Let's not take credit for anything, let's not make judgments. It all goes to God (CSG 161).

~

The artist's brush is nothing without the hand of the artist, and the work created is that of the artist alone. Lord, I place myself in your hands, guided by you, to do your marvelous work. As your trained disciple, make me an enlightened guide for my brothers and sisters.

"Each tree is known by its own fruit....The good person out of the good treasure of the heart produces good...for it is out of the abundance of the heart that the mouth speaks" (Lk 6:44–45).

~

[To a little child]—Dazzling deeds are forbidden to him, he can't preach the Gospel, shed his blood...but what does [it] matter? His brothers work in his place and he, the little child, stays close to the throne of the king and queen; he loves in the place of his brothers who go out and fight (Ms B, 4r).

~

Isn't love the treasure of a heart; isn't it what overflows from a generous and righteous heart? Only a child loves without measure. Lord, keep me like a child at heart who only wants to make the Father happy and help each one of your children bear the fruit of love.

Twenty-Fourth Sunday in Ordinary Time

"Then the father said to him, 'Son, you are always with me, and all that is mine is yours. But we had to celebrate and rejoice, because this brother of yours was dead and has come to life; he was lost and has been found'" (Lk 15:31–32).

~

Oh Jesus, your little bird is happy to be weak and small, but what would it become if it was big?...It will never have the boldness to appear in your presence, to nap before you (Ms B, 5r).

~

It is invigorating to hear you tell me I am always with you, even when I nap. I sleep but my heart is awake. I know my weaknesses, I know my smallness. Nevertheless, you are there to make me live again in you and include me in your joy. Lord, always remind me of your presence.

A centurion there had a slave whom he valued highly, and who was ill and close to death....."Lord, do not trouble yourself, for I am not worthy to have you come under my roof" (Lk 7:2–6).

~

Don't believe that [your child] puts a higher value on dying at dawn rather than at dusk. She only wants to please Jesus. (...) For a long time she has understood that God needs no one (her even less than others) to do good on earth (Ms C, 3r–v).

~

Lord, it is true; you don't need me to do your work and yet you call upon me to serve in your presence. No matter how long I serve or the importance of my service, as long as I am of service, Lord, let me be your servant.

Twenty-Fourth Tuesday in Ordinary Time

A man who had died was being carried out. He was his mother's only son, and she was a widow....And he [Jesus] said, "Young man, I say to you, rise!" The dead man sat up (Lk 7:12, 14–15).

~

It is toward you, oh Jesus, that my soul sighs. I have only one desire; it's to see you, Oh my Lord. I want to take my cross, gentle Savior, and follow you. I want nothing more than to die for your love. I want to die to begin to live. I want to die to unite myself with Jesus (RP 3).

~

The more spiritual a human is, the more the desire to see your beauty deepens. But full participation in your life will only be granted at the time of our death. Keep the desire deep in me to unite myself with you, in the solid assurance of the time when, at your call, I will rise from the dead.

"Nevertheless, wisdom is vindicated by all her children" (Lk 7:35).

～

Jesus knew that his little flower needed the life-giving water of humiliation. She was too weak to take root without this help (Ms C, 1v).

～

You who are the wisdom of God went all the way to the humiliation on the cross because of your love for the Father and for us. You call me to follow this same road of radical self-sacrifice to root myself deeply in your redemptive love and be invigorated by it. Lord, let me hear your wisdom.

She [the sinner] stood behind him at his feet, weeping, and began to bathe his feet with her tears and to dry them with her hair. Then she continued kissing his feet and anointing them with the ointment (Lk 7:38).

~

I gain no merit for having avoided the love of worldly things since I was saved from it only by the great mercy of God. I recognized that without him I could have fallen as low as Mary Magdalene, and the profound words of Our Lord to Simon entered my soul with a great gentleness (Ms A, 38v).

~

Lord, your forgiveness redeems all sinners who open themselves and believe in your love, regardless of their sins. Happy are those you saved from being torn apart. Happy are those you keep in the gentleness of your heart. Happy are those who use the strength of your love to support their weakness. Lord, I am a sinner, forgive me.

The twelve were with him, as well as some women who had been cured of evil spirits and infirmities (Lk 8:1–2).

⁓

The great saints worked for the glory of God, but since I am only a very small soul, I work to please him, for his "whims." (…) There are enough people who want to be useful! My dream is to be a frivolous toy in the hand of the Child Jesus....I am a plaything for the little Jesus! (CSG 57).

⁓

One can appreciate the company of someone by choice, in gratitude, or in support. Jesus, that is what gives me, in exchange, the honor to follow you, like a little child, to please you as you see fit, along the unpredictable road of life. Lord, this way, we will deepen our bond.

"But as for that in the good soil, these are the ones who, when they hear the word, hold it fast in an honest and good heart and bear fruit with patient endurance" (Lk 8:15).

~

My heavenly protectors and favorites are those who stole their way to heaven, like the Holy Innocents, and the good thief. The big saints won their places in heaven by their deeds, but I want to imitate the thieves; I want to have it through craftiness, the craftiness of love that will open the door to heaven to me and to the poor sinners (CSG 41).

~

If I don't show skillfulness and intelligence, how will I be able to improve my home soil to receive the word? If my know-how is not energized by love, what will happen to the fruit? Lord, in your kingdom, the ripe fruit will come from you and will be for you, unless I steal it, by a trickery of love, only to give it back to you as a gift of love.

Twenty-Fifth Sunday in Ordinary Time

"Whoever is faithful in a very little is faithful also in much"
(Lk 16:10).

~

If a canvas painted by an artist could think and speak, it could certainly not complain about being constantly touched and retouched by a paintbrush (...) because it would know that it wasn't the paintbrush, but the artist who guides it and to whom it owes the beauty with which it has been bestowed. The paintbrush, for its part, could not take credit for the masterpiece made by it. (...) I am a little paintbrush which Jesus chose to use to paint his image in the souls he has entrusted to me (Ms C, 20r).

~

To entrust an important task to someone is to have total confidence in them, one which grows with time. Lord, that is what you do by putting the paintbrush into my hands, to paint your image of beauty into the hearts of my brothers and sisters. Lord, guide my hand.

Twenty-Fifth Monday in Ordinary Time

"Then pay attention to how you listen" (Lk 8:18).

~

You are wrong to want the whole world to bend to your way of seeing things. We want to be little children and since...they don't know what is best, they find everything good: let us follow their example. There is no merit in doing what is reasonable, it is the common way; everyone in the world wants to follow it (CSG 185–186).

~

If we impose our own way of thinking and seeing things on others, we are not truly hearing what they say to us. To truly hear someone, we must let them speak, without saying a word, to let them leave the ordinary and follow a new way. Lord, help me be a good listener so others can find the new way to you.

Twenty-Fifth Tuesday in Ordinary Time

"My mother and my brothers are those who hear the word of God and do it" (Lk 8:21).

~

I applied myself to loving God, and...I understood that my love had to go beyond just words, because "it is not those who say: 'Lord, Lord!' who will enter the kingdom of heaven, but those who do the will of God" (Ms C, 11v).

∼

Son of God, if you adopt me as your brother to unite me closely with you, for my part, I need to have the trust of both a child and a brother. Upon hearing your word in my heart, my path is lit, and I will be able to bond with you in a response of love. Lord, be with me.

Twenty-Fifth Wednesday in Ordinary Time

[Jesus] sent them [the twelve apostles] out to proclaim the kingdom of God and to heal (Lk 9:2).

∼

I hoped that the kingdom of Carmel would be mine soon. I did not think of these other words of Jesus: "I prepare my kingdom for you as my Father prepared it for me." That is to say, I am keeping crosses and trials for you so that you will be worthy to have this kingdom you desire (Ms A, 62v).

∼

Jesus, the cross was a heavy burden which you could only live through by love. Through it, the doors of the kingdom of glory open to all humanity. Your path is also mine. By living it in hope, may I become a herald for your love.

Twenty-Fifth Thursday in Ordinary Time

Herod said, "John I beheaded; but who is this about whom I hear such things?" And he tried to see him (Lk 9:9).

~

Close to your divine Heart, I forget all that happens. I no longer dread the fears of the night. Oh Jesus! give me a place in this heart If only for today (PN 5).

~

There is quite a difference between hearing someone speak about another and knowing them, but one can lead to the other. In this same way, you invite me to come with you and open your heart to me. Close to you, I have no fears. Every day, you let me enjoy your loving presence in the hope of seeing you. Lord, increase my closeness to you.

Twenty-Fifth Friday in Ordinary Time

"The Son of Man must undergo great suffering, and be rejected by the elders, chief priests, and scribes, and be killed, and on the third day be raised" (Lk 9:22).

~

This pathway [of pain] has been mine for the past five years. But on the outside, nothing showed my suffering, which made it even more painful because I was the only one to know it (Ms A, 70r).

~

Jesus, suffering will always be a mystery. You see it as an inflexible reality, and you will carry it alone because your friends did not understand. How many after you will know the painful solitude of suffering? For it not to show, they would need a certain strength of character and a good many blessings! Lord, help me in my suffering.

Twenty-Fifth Saturday in Ordinary Time

"Let these words sink into your ears: The Son of Man is going to be betrayed into human hands" (Lk 9:44).

~

I see that only suffering can deliver life to souls. More than ever, these sublime words of Jesus unveil their depth to me: "In truth I say to you, if this wheat seed that fell in the soil doesn't die, it will live alone, but if it dies, it will produce many fruit" (Ms A, 81r).

~

Isn't our birth a result of the pain of childbirth? Isn't all life preceded by a stage that seems to be like death? Yet life finally wins. Lord, may I learn from you the value of the death of the seed so I can live in you.

"The poor man [Lazarus] died and was carried away by the angels to be with Abraham. The rich man also died and was buried" (Lk 16:22).

~

Let us look at life in its true light....It is but a moment between two eternities....Let us suffer in peace....I confess that this word "peace" seemed a little strong, but whoever said "peace" did not say "joy" or, at least, "the feeling of joy."...To suffer in peace, it is enough to want all that Jesus wants....To be the bride of Jesus, one must be like Jesus, covered with blood, crowned with thorns (LT 87).

~

Lord, humankind must work today to have a future in you. Made for living, may humanity never die. Lord, give me meaning for my life and profound peace with inner joy. Make me act in accordance with your will.

"Whoever welcomes this child in my name welcomes me"
(Lk 9:48).

∿

In the religious community, there is a Sister who dis-
pleases me in all that she does, her mannerisms, her
words, her character seem disagreeable to me. However,
she is a holy religious who must be very acceptable to
God, so not wanting to yield to the natural antipathy I
felt, I told myself that charity shouldn't concern feelings,
but deeds (Ms C, 13v).

∿

I must go beyond my feelings if I am to accept someone for
what they are and succeed in seeing them in Jesus. No
doubt, I will have to overcome my misgivings. A charitable welcome will always go beyond feelings and preju-
dices. Lord, help me to accept people as they are.

Twenty-Sixth Tuesday in Ordinary Time

When the days drew near for him to be taken up, he set his face to go to Jerusalem. And he sent messengers ahead of him (Lk 9:51–52).

~

Jesus…wants us to join him in the salvation of souls. He wants to do nothing without us. The creator of the universe awaits the prayer of a poor little soul to save the other souls, redeemed like it, at the price of his blood. (…)Isn't the apostolate of prayer of more value than that of simple words? (LT 135).

~

You send me as a poor herald on the road of your redeeming love. This poverty is, in fact, my strength. Your work in me, by the blood of your cross, is my salvation. Through prayer, you make me your messenger for the salvation of my brothers and sisters. Power to the prayer of the poor!

Twenty-Sixth Wednesday in Ordinary Time

As they were going along the road, someone said to him [Jesus], "I will follow you wherever you go" (Lk 9:57).

~

I am not afraid to live a long life, I don't refuse to fight. (…) Also, I never asked God to die young, but it is true,

I always hoped this to be his will. Often, God is satisfied with the desire to work for his glory, and you know that my desires are very great (Ms C, 8v).

~

Jesus, you call me to walk your path, to follow you with an enthusiastic desire to work for you and to develop wisdom as time passes. Lord, put great desires into my heart so that I will work for your glory.

Twenty-Sixth Thursday in Ordinary Time

"Go on your way. See, I am sending you out like lambs into the midst of wolves" (Lk 10:3).

~

My beloved Mother, I told you, my last recourse so as not to be conquered in battle is to walk away from the fight. I have already used this method during my novitiate, and it always worked perfectly. (…) I believe it is better not to expose oneself to the fight when defeat is certain! (Ms C, 14v–15r).

~

Desertion in combat is cowardice. But faced with a spiritual battle stronger than I am, it is better to leave. Besides, are you not sending me into battle like a defenseless lamb, the symbol of sacrifice? Lord, keep me capable of the effort without tiring, but also without presumption.

Twenty-Sixth Friday in Ordinary Time

"Whoever listens to you listens to me, and whoever rejects you rejects me, and whoever rejects me rejects the one who sent me" (Lk 10:16).

~

From afar, it seems like a perfect way to do good for souls and to make them love God more is to shape them using your own personal views and thoughts. But up close, it is just the opposite; it is not so perfect. (...) One feels that one must absolutely lose one's own perceptions and personal opinions and guide souls using the path Jesus laid out for them, without trying to make them walk in his actual path (Ms C, 22v).

~

The messenger is always the spokesperson for someone else, not for himself. Nevertheless, his own testimony reflects upon him. Lord, may I hear you before I proclaim you to my brothers and sisters, and then give up my own personal views. In this way, I will be able to guide others on their own pathways, mindful of your love.

Twenty-Sixth Saturday in Ordinary Time

The seventy returned with joy....Jesus rejoiced in the Holy Spirit (Lk 10:17–21).

~

The Almighty gave the saints a solid foundation to lean on: himself and only him; as a lever: prayer, which ignites with the fire of love. This is how they excited the world. That is how the saints who are still active are doing it and that is how, until the end time, all the saints to come will also do it (Ms C, 36v).

~

How can an apostle excite the world and still know inner joy? By being a person of prayer who leans on the teacher, Jesus. As for discouragement, he never reaches that point, as long as he allows himself to be invigorated by the Holy Spirit and ignited by its love. That's what enlightens me to excite the world. Lord, make me a person of prayer.

"When you have done all that you were ordered to do, say, 'We are worthless slaves; we have done only what we ought to have done!'" (Lk 17:10).

~

But how can the little child show his love, since love is proven by good deeds? Oh well, the little child will throw flowers. (…) That is to say, to not let a single chance go by for a small sacrifice, not a glance, not a word, to take advantage of all the little things and to do them out of love (Ms B, 4r–v).

~

It hardly seems glorious to be an ordinary servant. Nevertheless, he fulfills duties of all types, some often thankless. Lord, this is what you expect from me: that I put love into the littlest things which make up my regular duties, and that I prove my love for you. Lord, help me do all that I do through love.

"Which of these three, do you think, was a neighbor to the man who fell into the hands of the robbers?" He [the lawyer] said, "The one who showed him mercy" (Lk 10:36–37).

~

I understood that charity must not remain locked up in one's heart: Jesus said, "No one lights a candlestick to put it under a bushel; we put it in a chandelier, so that it lights up all those who are in the house." It seems to me that this candlestick represents charity which should shed light on and delight not only those people who are dearest to me, but ALL those in the house, without exception (Ms C, 12r).

~

It's fine to have good ideas and unselfish feelings, but charity must be shown in my life until I become a neighbor to anyone in need. It should be a resourceful charity that comforts, appeases, and gives hope back to others. The well from which I drink is you, Lord; quench my thirst.

Mary...sat at the Lord's feet and listened to what he was saying. But Martha was distracted by her many tasks (Lk 10:39–40).

∽

The priests, the most ardent Christians, find that we are excessive, that we should serve like Martha, instead of dedicating our lives [like vases filled with perfume] to Jesus....However, it is not important that our vases are broken, since Jesus is comforted; and in spite of him, the world must smell the perfumes which escape and purify the poisoned air that it keeps breathing (LT 169).

∽

Why are there consecrated men and women living silently in cloisters? Lord, they are there to offer you the best of themselves, their thirst to love and dedicate themselves to serve the Church. But they are also there for humanity, so that it will inhale the peace and inner joy of the cloisters and be capable of divine listening. Lord, bless these men and women.

"Lord, teach us to pray....He said to them, 'When you pray, say: Father...'" (Lk 11:1–2).

~

[To pray]—I do it like the children who don't know how to read. I simply tell God what I want to, without fancy words, and he always understands me....For me, prayer is a burst from my heart, it is a simple glance thrown toward heaven, a cry of thanksgiving and love in times of trial as well as in times of joy. Finally, it is something big, supernatural, which opens up my soul and unites me with Jesus (Ms C, 25r–v).

~

Because my prayer is woven into the tight fabric of my life, it is sometimes a cry of joy or distress, sometimes a recognition of love or a call for help in a time of trial, sometimes adoration or a request for blessings and forgiveness. But it is always a burst from my heart, sent to you, the Father. Lord, hear my prayer.

Twenty-Seventh Thursday in Ordinary Time

"If you then, who are evil, know how to give good gifts to your children, how much more will the heavenly Father give the Holy Spirit to those who ask him!" (Lk 11:13).

~

I owe my gentlest joys and strongest impressions which excited me to practice virtue to the pretty pictures you showed me as a reward (Ms A, 31v).

~

The beauty of your creation, like humankind's masterpieces, impress and mold me, making me look upon the world with a glance filled with wonder. Father, by the gift of your Spirit, transform this glance into a spiritual lifting-up.

Twenty-Seventh Friday in Ordinary Time

"But if it is by the finger of God that I cast out the demons, then the kingdom of God has come to you" (Lk 11:20).

~

At the beginning, my face often betrayed the battle, but little by little, this disappeared and renunciation became easier for me, even from the first instance. For each faithfully received blessing, Jesus granted a multitude of others to me (Ms A, 48r–v).

~

Lord, I must fight continuously to open my heart to you, to let myself be freed by you from the power of evil. No one other than the two of us sees this. Otherwise, what good would it be? My faithfulness to your first blessing brings into me the kingdom of your kindness, which is a source of a multitude of blessings. Lord, may I always be faithful.

Twenty-Seventh Saturday in Ordinary Time

"Blessed is the womb that bore you and the breasts that nursed you!" (Lk 11:27).

∼

All alone, saying the rosary requires an effort for me. I feel that I say it so badly! Even if I strained to meditate on the mysteries of the rosary, I can't concentrate....I was distressed for a long time over this lack of devotion which surprised me, since I love the Blessed Virgin Mary so much. (…) Now I am less distressed, because I think that the Queen of Heaven, being my mother, must see my goodwill and is satisfied by it (Ms C, 25v).

∼

Blessed Virgin Mary, at times I am clumsy when telling you of my love, but you can go beyond appearances to see the signs of love. You are happy to see me saying the rosary, even if my mind wanders a little, because I remind you of your supreme blessing: to have been the mother of his only Son. Hail Mary, full of grace.

Then Jesus asked, "Were not ten [lepers] made clean? But the other nine, where are they? Was none of them found to return and give praise to God except this foreigner?" (Lk 17:17–18).

~

I cannot say that I had received solace often during my acts of thanksgiving. It was perhaps the time when I received the least....I find that to be normal, seeing that I offered myself to Jesus, not as a person who wanted to receive him for my own solace, but just the opposite, to please the One who gives himself to me (Ms A, 79v).

~

Jesus, how great your heart must suffer when faced with the sons of the covenant who don't return your blessings. But you never waited for exterior solace. Your only comfort has been the Father, to whom your whole life was an act of thanksgiving. My true solace is in you, to whom I devote myself, beyond feelings. Lord, I praise you and offer my humble thanks.

"The people of Nineveh will rise up at the judgment with this generation and condemn it, because they repented at the proclamation of Jonah" (Lk 11:32).

~

So that a reprimand brings fruit, it must cost dearly to do it and not have even a shadow of anger in the heart (CSG 8).

~

It is a fraternal duty to point out shortcomings and flaws. It goes without saying, it must be done with tact and respect. The person who accepts these remarks takes the costly road to repentance. Lord, may I know how to give as well as receive a reprimand.

"You fools! Did not the one who made the outside make the inside also?" (Lk 11:40).

~

An artist doesn't use only one paintbrush; he needs at least two. The first is the more useful because it is used to apply the overall tones which cover the entire canvas in a very short time. The other one, which is smaller, is used to paint the details. My Mother, you are the precious paintbrush seized by the hand of Jesus out of love when he wants to do big things in the souls of his children. I am the smaller one which he deigns to use afterwards, for the minor details (Ms C, 20r–v).

~

I am entirely your work since all creation exists only through you, and nothing is foreign to you. You paint my inner self with such talent, touching up the details with the little paintbrush of your love so that I will truly be "me." Thank you, Lord.

"Woe also to you lawyers! For you load people with burdens hard to bear, and you yourselves do not lift a finger to ease them" (Lk 11:46).

～

We would like to never fall. Jesus, what does it matter if I fall constantly? That is how I see my weakness, and for me, this is a big benefit. Through it, you see what I can do and will now be more inclined to carry me in your arms....If you don't, it is because it pleases you to see me on the ground....Then, I will not worry, but I will always extend my arms to you, beseeching and full of love (LT 89).

～

Lord, to do the impossible is out of my reach and you don't expect it of me. I fall under the added burdens of life, whether they are of my own creation or as a result of my weakness. I know that I will not be able to pick myself up or continue on without you. See my arms extended to you in need of support. Lord, be my support.

"Woe to you....For you have taken away the key of knowledge; you did not enter yourselves, and you hindered those who were entering" (Lk 11:52).

～

I told you that (...) I learned a great deal by teaching others. First, I saw that all souls have essentially the same battles; but on the other hand, they are so very different that I have no trouble understanding what Father Pichon said: "There are more differences between souls than there are between faces." Also, it is impossible to act the same with all of them (Ms C, 23v).

～

A key only unlocks one lock because each is unique. I should always respect the key to each person's knowledge so I can discover their individual personality. At the same time, I will have to open their horizons without overlooking the differences. This forces me to have intellectual flexibility, selflessness, and an opening to the Spirit. Lord, help me be open to others.

"Are not five sparrows sold for two pennies? Yet not one of them is forgotten in God's sight....Do not be afraid; you are of more value than many sparrows" (Lk 12:6–7).

～

Jesus is satisfied to make me feel humble, deep in my soul. To human eyes, everything works for me. (...) I understand that I must walk this dangerous road, not for myself, but for others. In effect, if I appear, in the eyes of the community, to be a religious full of faults and incapable, without intelligence or judgment, it would be impossible, Mother, for you to request my help. That is why God has thrown a veil over my flaws, both inner and exterior (Ms C, 26v).

～

Lord, if you did not veil my shortcomings, I would be as insignificant as a sparrow. As you want me to be of service to others, you bless me with strength and know-how. But, deep in my soul, I must remain humble. Lord, show me how to best serve you.

"For the Holy Spirit will teach you at that very hour what you ought to say" (Lk 12:12).

~

In order to love you like you love me, I must borrow your own love, and only then do I find rest. Oh Jesus, maybe it is an illusion, but it seems you can't give a soul more love than you've given mine. It is for this reason I dare to ask you to love those who you have given me in the same way as you have loved me (Ms C, 35r).

~

Lord, thanks to the Holy Spirit, I can see how much I am loved by you. By the words the Holy Spirit inspires in me, I can tell you of my own love. By this gift, I become able to love those you have given me as brothers and sisters. Lord, continue to teach me about love.

"And will not God grant justice to his chosen ones who cry to him day and night?…He will quickly grant justice to them" (Lk 18:7–8).

~

I know that one must be very pure to appear before the God of all holiness, but I also know that the Lord is infinitely just. It is this justice which is the subject of my joy and confidence. To be just is not only to be strict in punishing the guilty, it is also to recognize righteous intentions and reward virtue. I expect as much from God's justice as from his mercy (LT 226).

~

You are the God who judges the lives of the chosen ones who cry out to you. Because you are the Father, you grant them some of your own holiness by showing them mercy. You do not terrorize your children, you save them. Lord, I trust in your justice as in your mercy.

Twenty-Ninth Monday in Ordinary Time

"Take care! Be on your guard against all kinds of greed; for one's life does not consist in the abundance of possessions" (Lk 12:15).

~

Why look for happiness on earth? I confess that my heart has a passionate thirst for it, but this poor heart also sees clearly that no human is able to quench its thirst. (...) I knew another wellspring, the one where, once having drank from it, one is still thirsty, but not with an impatient thirst; just the opposite, with a very gentle one, because it has something to satisfy it. This wellspring is the suffering known only to Jesus (LT 75).

~

Nothing is completely or truly satisfying on earth, as everything is so fleeting. Where will I be able to quench my thirst for happiness? By taking small sips of life each day, with its mixture of joys and sorrows, and by offering it to you, Lord Jesus, in the secrecy of my heart, and by staying thirsty for the true wealth of you. Lord, keep me away from greed.

Twenty-Ninth Tuesday in Ordinary Time

"Be dressed for action and have your lamps lit" (Lk 12:35).

～

A painter who works for his master doesn't have to say at each brush stroke: this is for this certain person or that other. (...) It is enough to go to work with the will to work for his master. It is a good idea for him to gather his thoughts often and redirect his intentions without any constraints on his mind. Our Lord guesses the nice thoughts and inventive intentions we would like to have. He is the Father, and we are his little children (CSG 45).

～

Lord, you call me to work for the kingdom. I serve by doing my regular duties and by orienting my will to serve you in the freedom of the spirit. I serve with the simplicity of my childlike heart, by living in your presence, my Father. Lord, show me how to serve you.

"From everyone to whom much has been given, much will be required; and from the one to whom much has been entrusted, even more will be demanded" (Lk 12:48).

～

Don't believe that humility prevents me from recognizing God's gifts. I know that he works big things in me and I happily sing his praises each day. I remember that the one who has received more must love more. Also I work in such a way so as to make my life an act of love. I no longer worry about being a small soul; just the opposite, I am thrilled by it (LT 224).

～

Lord, I glorify you by recognizing the talents I have received from you. You have given me a great deal, so when it is my turn, I will give generously with love. This doesn't stop me from knowing that I am small before you. Precisely, through my smallness, it is obvious that my talents come from you. Lord, help me give generously.

Twenty-Ninth Thursday in Ordinary Time

"I came to bring fire to the earth, and how I wish it were already kindled!" (Lk 12:49).

~

Jesus prefers to leave me in the dark rather than giving me a false glimmer which would not be him! Since I can't find any human who pleases me, I want to give everything to Jesus. I don't want to give just a bit of my love to someone. May Jesus always make me understand that he alone is perfect happiness, even when he seems absent! (LT 76).

~

It is better to be left in the dark than to let myself be drawn in by false glimmers like pleasure, money, superiority, and appearances…which can't fulfill me anyway. Jesus, if your consuming love enflames my heart, I will discover that you alone are the bright light in my life. Lord, kindle your fire in me.

"You know how to interpret the appearance of earth and sky, but why do you not know how to interpret the present time?" (Lk 12:56).

～

On the way back, I looked up at the gently twinkling stars and this sight delighted me....There, I joyfully noticed a group of these golden pearls in the shape of a T. I pointed it out to Papa and told him that my name was written in heaven (Ms A, 18r).

～

Stars only sparkle in the serene sky of a blue-tinted night. Bright spots, symbols of the many lights that dot my darkness. Bright spots which draw my glance towards God's heaven where my name is written. This star-studded canopy of heaven represents those who are united in you, Lord. Teach me to see and understand this in faith.

"See here! For three years I have come looking for fruit on this fig tree, and still I find none. Cut it down! Why should it be wasting the soil?" He replied, "Sir, let it alone for one more year" (Lk 13:7–8).

~

One must never believe when you don't practice virtue that it is due to a natural cause, like illness, the weather, or grief. You should feel great humiliation from it and put yourself in with the little souls, since you can practice virtue only in a very weak way (CSG 22).

~

It is so much easier for me to apologize than to look for the real reasons for my fruitlessness. But, then, I cannot keep my place in the fertile soil of the Church. Lord, open my heart to generosity; forgive me for being so weak when faced with difficulties; let me be hope for fruitful achievement of your glory.

"The Pharisee, standing by himself, was praying....But the tax collector, standing far off,...was beating his breast and saying, 'God, be merciful to me, a sinner!'...For all who exalt themselves will be humbled, but all who humble themselves will be exalted" (Lk 18:11, 13–14).

~

I don't seek the first place, but the last. Instead of standing up with the Pharisee, I repeat, full of confidence, the humble prayer of the tax collector. But above all, I imitate the behavior of Mary Magdalene. Her surprising, or rather, loving boldness, which charms the heart of Jesus, captivates mine (Ms C, 36v).

~

Jesus, I kneel at your feet, in last place, begging your forgiveness with the assurance that you hear my cry and will come to save me from the force of evil. With the boldness of love, Lord, I beg for your gentle mercy for all sinners.

And just then there appeared a woman....She was bent over and was quite unable to stand up straight....When he [Jesus] laid his hands on her, immediately she stood up straight and began praising God (Lk 13:11–13).

~

I am much happier to have been imperfect than if, supported by grace, I had been a model of gentleness.... It made me feel so much better to see that Jesus is always so gentle and tender toward me! Oh, from now on, I will recognize it; yes, all my hopes will be fulfilled....Yes, the Lord will make marvels for us which will infinitely surpass our great desires (LT 230).

~

Lord, because of my shortcomings and sins, I approach you and bow before you. Needing no words, my action is enough for you and shows my deep desire to rediscover myself upright, ready to serve you. Lord, your hand placed on me will fulfill my hope.

"It is like a mustard seed that someone took and sowed in the garden; it grew and became a tree, and the birds of the air made nests in its branches" (Lk 13:19).

~

The zeal of a Carmelite must include the whole world. (…) I could not forget to pray for all the missionaries as well as the simple priests, whose mission is sometimes as difficult to fulfill as that of the apostles, preaching to the unfaithful. Finally, I want to be a daughter of the Church (…) and pray with the same intentions as our Holy Father, the pope, knowing that his intentions encompass the universe. That is the overall goal of my life (Ms C, 33v).

~

Since I am a little seed in God's field, how can I know the extent of the apostolate? We can know the extent by being sons and daughters of the Church attentive to all that makes up its life; by joining our hearts to those who carry on a ministry; and by praying fervently for the servants of the Gospel. Lord, help this little seed grow into a tree.

Thirtieth Wednesday in Ordinary Time

"Then people will come from east and west, from north and south, and will eat in the kingdom of God" (Lk 13:29).

~

Jesus is happy to show me the only path to the divine blazing fire. This path is the self-abandon of the little child who sleeps without fear in his father's arms. (…) Oh, if all the weak and imperfect souls felt what the soul of your little Thérèse feels, not a single one would lose hope to reach the peak of the mountain of love, since Jesus doesn't ask for big deeds, but simply self-abandon and gracious recognition (LT 196).

~

Lord Jesus, you have opened the way to the kingdom, which the immense crowd of redeemed souls have undertaken. The ascent toward the divine horizon is difficult, but you support and draw to you whoever recognizes you and puts themselves into your hands. Lord, you are the only path to the Father.

"Yet today, tomorrow, and the next day I must be on my way, because it is impossible for a prophet to be killed outside of Jerusalem" (Lk 13:33).

～

Sometimes a great desire to hear something other than praise comes to me. You know(...)I prefer vinegar over sugar. My soul also tires of the nourishment that is too sweet, and then, at that time, Jesus lets us serve him a little salad, well-seasoned with vinegar, very spicy; nothing is missing except the oil (Ms C, 26v–27r).

～

Jesus, my path as a disciple could only just resemble yours, seasoned with the salt of harshness and the vinegar of all adversaries. The sweetness of praise also tires me. It is with this same nourishment that I must continue on this path, today and tomorrow. You walk ahead, I will follow.

"Is it lawful to cure people on the sabbath, or not?" But they were silent (Lk 14:3–4).

~

Oh, I feel it; Jesus is even thirstier than ever! He only encounters thankless and indifferent people among his followers and disciples. Alas, among his disciples, he find few hearts given to him without reservation and who understand the tenderness of his infinite love (LT 196).

~

Some silences show ingratitude and cowardice. Lord, we can't follow you without committing ourselves to you and for you. Forgive me for all my excessive reservations, for my unimaginative silences, and for my ignorance of your redemptive love.

"Those who humble themselves will be exalted" (Lk 14:11).

～

As soon as God sees us truly convinced of our nothing-ness, he extends his hand to us. If we again want to try to do something big, even under the pretense of zeal, Jesus leaves us alone. (...) Yes, it is enough to humble oneself and endure our imperfections with gentleness. That is true holiness (LT 243).

～

To imagine we can, on our own, stand up and struggle to climb the mountain of holiness, is a sure way to find our-selves lying flat on the ground. To begin the climb to holi-ness, we must recognize and endure our limitations, make ourselves very small and take the hand that God extends to us. Lord, extend your hand.

Zacchaeus stood there and said to the Lord, "Look, half of my possessions, Lord, I will give to the poor; and if I have defrauded anyone of anything, I will pay back four times as much." Then Jesus said to him, "Today salvation has come to this house" (Lk 19:8–9).

～

Often, the soul isn't strong enough to bear praise. It must, then, at times, sacrifice an obvious possession for its own sanctification. You should be delighted to fall, for if falling did not offend God, we would have to do it on purpose, in order to humble ourselves (CSG 27).

～

Lord, how can I meet you in truth without ridding myself of the fleeting goods of life? But this doesn't happen without a fight, maybe even a fall. Beyond humiliation, I can feel this divesting will become, thanks to you, a path for sanctification and salvation. Lord, help me rid myself of useless possessions.

"But when you give a banquet, invite the poor....And you will be blessed, because they cannot repay you" (Lk 14:13–14).

~

When I don't have the opportunity [to please Jesus], I want to at least tell him often that I love him. It is not difficult, and it maintains the fire. Even if I would feel that this fire of love would be extinguished, I would like to throw something into it, and Jesus would surely rekindle it (LT 143).

~

An invitation brings us out of ourselves by opening ourselves to the guest. And in our guest, there is always a certain need to fill. Make me know how to discover that need. Then, Lord, let yourself be revealed in that person. That way, my charity will find strength again. Lord, let me tender the invitation to you often.

Thirty-First Tuesday in Ordinary Time

"At the time for the dinner he sent his slave to say to those who had been invited, 'Come; for everything is ready now.' But they all alike began to make excuses" (Lk 14:17–18).

~

I also have weaknesses, but I am thrilled to have them. I don't always set myself above the little nothings of this world, if, for example, I would be teased for a silly thing I said or did. At that time, I withdraw into myself and think: Alas, I'm still back at the same point as before! But I tell myself this with a great deal of tenderness and without sadness. It is so sweet to feel oneself weak and small (DE 5.7.1).

~

Lord, I ignore your invitations because of my current worries and when the "nothings" of the world overtake me. I could be saddened and upset over this. I prefer to show you my weakness and, in this way, I will touch your Father's heart and you will take me with you. Lord, may I accept more of your invitations.

Thirty-First Wednesday in Ordinary Time

"Whoever comes to me and does not hate father and mother, wife and children, brothers and sisters, yes, and even life itself, cannot be my disciple" (Lk 14:26).

~

It is true that there are very large and heavy crosses in the world....Those in religious life are daily prods, the fight is practiced on a completely different plane. One must fight against oneself, to destroy one's inner self. It is through this that one garners true victories. (...) I noticed here that the seemingly strongest characters were, in these little things, the easiest to defeat. It is so very true that our greatest victories are those when we conquer ourselves (CSG 149).

~

For me to detach myself from my earthly environment already requires a great sacrifice. It will cost me much more to conquer my sense of self in all things, in order to be totally yours, Lord Jesus. Be my living strength.

Thirty-First Thursday in Ordinary Time

"There will be more joy in heaven over one sinner who repents than over ninety-nine righteous persons who need no repentance" (Lk 15:7).

~

Pranzini had not [yet] confessed [but] (...) seized by a sudden inspiration, he turned around, grabbed a crucifix that the priest was offering him and kissed its holy wounds three times!...Then his soul went on to receive a merciful sentence from the One who declares that there is more joy in heaven for one single sinner who repents his sins than for ninety-nine righteous people who do not need repentance (Ms A, 46r).

~

Prayer is all-powerful when it springs forth from a humble, confident heart. Lord, you expect it from your children in order to grant mercy to the sinners who seize your loving call in a thundering flash of light, or while along the road to repentance, or in the glimmer of their last moments of life. From now on, the cross will shine forever on the world, as a sign of salvation.

"The children of this age are more shrewd in dealing with their own generation than are the children of light" (Lk 16:8).

~

I am always happy. I fix it so that even in the midst of a storm, I keep calm inside. If someone tells me of disagreements with the Sisters, I try not to get upset with this person or that one. It is necessary, for example, while I listen, for me to look out the window and silently enjoy the sight of the sky and the trees (DE 18.4.1).

~

To keep one's serenity in the midst of storms requires great self control and the use of some means of diversion. To be involved in such a situation but, at the same time, to look at something outside that makes one internalize another reality, is the talent given to the sons and daughters of the light. Lord, help me to be serene is all situations.

"Whoever is faithful in a very little is faithful also in much" (Lk 16:10).

~

To be small is, once again, not to take credit for the virtues one practices or believing oneself capable of doing something, but recognizing that God places this treasure into the hands of his little child so he can use it when he needs to, but it is always God's treasure. Finally, one mustn't be discouraged with one's mistakes, as children fall often, but they are too small to injure themselves badly (DE 6.8.8).

~

Lord, you trust me by putting the treasure that you are into my hand. You, the love of plenitude, do this so that I can live in this treasure. Yet I don't deserve this trust, as I am a sinner. Even the good I do comes from you and not from me. I am only a little one, your child, who leans totally on you alone. Lord, make me worthy.

"Those who are considered worthy of a place in that age and in the resurrection from the dead neither marry nor are given in marriage. Indeed they cannot die anymore, because they are like angels and are children of God, being children of the resurrection" (Lk 20:35–36).

⌣

I would like to tell you what I mean by the scent of the Beloved's perfume. Since Jesus has returned to heaven, I can only follow him by the tracks he left, but these tracks are so bright and fragrant! I only have to direct my eyes to the holy Gospel and right away, I breathe in the perfume of the life of Jesus, and I know which way to run (Ms C, 36v).

⌣

I am truly an earthly being; spirit, soul, and body. Jesus, you took this form yourself. The Gospel, by revealing that I am a child of God, carries me toward the horizons of eternity. There, in the manner of the angels, in adoration and praise, you offer to satisfy me in the rapture of love. Lord, let me follow your tracks.

The apostles said to the Lord, "Increase our faith!" (Lk 17:5).

~

[On the evening of Good Friday], I enjoyed a faith so alive, so clear, that the thought of heaven was my entire happiness. I couldn't believe that there were ungodly people having no faith. I believed that they were speaking nonsense by denying the existence of heaven, of that beautiful heaven where God wanted to be their eternal reward (Ms C, 5r–v).

~

Blessed be the one whose trusting and enlightened faith lights the road of life. What interior strength for him in those heavy and painful hours of the Good Fridays of life. What a blessing it is to know where the road leads. Lord, hear my call; increase my faith.

Thirty-Second Tuesday in Ordinary Time

"We are worthless slaves; we have done only what we ought to have done!" (Lk 17:10).

~

Understand that to love Jesus, to be his victim of love, the more one is weak, without desires or virtues, the more one is ready for the workings of this burning, transforming love…. Just the desire to be a victim is enough, but we must agree to always remain poor and without strength. (…) Let us love our smallness, let us love until we feel nothing; then we will be poor in spirit and Jesus will come get us, no matter how far away we are and change us into flames of love (LT 197).

~

To look for respect and self-worth is more in the style of the day, rather than to accept and love our smallness and weakness. What consideration does the world give to a person who seems to have no particular value? Jesus, you revere the poor person who offers himself to your burning love without measure, and make him a "flame" of love. Lord, I want to be poor in spirit.

Ten lepers approached him. Keeping their distance, they called out, saying, "Jesus, Master, have mercy on us!" (Lk 17:12–13).

~

*Is there any greater joy than to suffer for your love?...
The more intimate the suffering is, the less evident it is to human eyes; and the more it delights you, oh my Lord! If the impossible happens and you ignore my suffering, I would still be happy to have it if, through it, I could prevent or repair even a single sin committed against faith (Ms C, 7r).*

~

An outcry of suffering is a liberating cry because we escape our self by calling out to another. Lord Jesus, we also carry suffering deep in our hearts—a suffering which we offer to be united with your own through love. Hear my call on those days when the burdens are too heavy. Receive my offering in times of courage.

"For as the lightning flashes and lights up the sky from one side to the other, so will the Son of Man be in his day. But first he must endure much suffering and be rejected by this generation" (Lk 17:24–25).

~

How few friends our Lord had when he kept silent before the judges! Oh, what a song Jesus' silence was for my heart!...He made himself poor so we could show him charity. He extends his hand to us like a beggar so that, on the radiant judgment day when he will appear in his glory, he can let us hear his gentle words—"Come, those who are blessed by my Father." Jesus himself said those words, he wants our love, he begs for it (LT 145).

~

Before the glorious day when the Son of Man could come, he had to endure his hour of agony, in solitude, in silence and suffering. It was an hour of supreme love in the midst of extreme poverty. You invite me to join in your hour, your blessed Passion, so that I know your day, in the vision of your glory. Lord, let me suffer with you.

"Those who try to make their life secure will lose it, but those who lose their life will keep it" (Lk 17:33).

～

I am ready to give my life for them [your little lambs], but my affection is so pure, I do not want them to know it. I have never used Jesus to try to draw their hearts to me. I understood that my mission was to lead them to God and make them understand that, down here on earth, you, my Mother, are the visible Jesus, whom they must love and respect (Ms C, 23v).

～

We must give up a part of ourselves to be the road to lead others to you, Lord, and to not claim them for ourselves. One can't achieve that without sacrifice and a certain carefulness of speech, so as not to stand in the way. Lord, this is the mission you give me, what I live for.

"Pray always and do not to lose heart" (Lk 18:1).

~

How great is the power of prayer! (...) It isn't necessary to read a nice formula for a particular circumstance from a book for it to be granted; if it was so...alas, how I should be pitied!...Outside of the Divine Office, which I am not worthy to recite, I don't have the courage to force myself to look for nice prayers in books; this gives me a headache, there are so many prayers;...and they are all so beautiful, each one nicer than the next (Ms C, 25r).

~

Spontaneous prayer only comes from a heart which is filled with love and accustomed to being nourished by the Word of God and by the praise of the Hours. These are rich sources that permit our ordinary daily life, work, and relationships to be transformed by prayer, so we can make our life become a courageous gift to Christ. Lord, make me a prayer.

"You will be betrayed even…by relatives and friends….But not a hair of your head will perish. By your endurance you will gain your souls" (Lk 21:16, 18–19).

~

No matter what makes the little reed bend, it isn't afraid of breaking because it was planted at the edge of the water. (…) Its weakness gives it confidence; it could not break, because no matter what happens to it, it can only see the gentle hand of Jesus….At times, the little gusts of wind are more unbearable to it than the great storms (LT 55).

~

I know my weakness, humble reed that I am, but I know that you watch over me, Lord. I push ahead, then, with confidence, on the road of life where your hand guides me. There are also little blows that hurt me even more because they come from where I would not expect them. Lord, I beg you, don't let them break me.

Thirty-Third Monday in Ordinary Time

A blind man was sitting by the roadside begging. Then he shouted, "Jesus, Son of David, have mercy on me!" Those who were in front sternly ordered him to be quiet; but he shouted even more loudly, "Son of David, have mercy on me!" Jesus stood still and ordered the man to be brought to him (Lk 18:35, 38–40).

~

He [Jesus] alone hears when nothing answers us....He alone lays out our life of exile. It is he who, at times, presents us with the bitter chalice. But we don't see him; he hides, he veils his divine hand and we can only see human ones. That makes us suffer, since the voice of the Beloved doesn't make itself heard and that of the humans seems to misunderstand us....Yes, the most bitter sorrow is not to be understood (LT 149).

~

Humankind tries to silence those who shout their problems loudly because it embarrasses them. They want to have a hand in it all. Lord, at times, you stay silent, as if you don't hear. However, I know you always stop before the person who suffers and cries out for you. Lord, may I hear the cries of others and take them to you.

Thirty-Third Tuesday in Ordinary Time

He [Zacchaeus] was trying to see who Jesus was....He climbed a sycamore tree to see him, because he was going to pass that way (Lk 19:3–4).

～

It is incredible how large my heart seems to be when I think of all the treasures on earth, since I see that all of them together could not satisfy it. But when I think about Jesus, how small it seems to me!...I would like to love him so much;...to love him more than he has ever been loved! My only desire is to always do the will of Jesus! (LT 74).

～

Jesus, Zacchaeus was too small to see you, but his heart was generous enough to repent and love you. My heart is too small to love you as you wish, but I have a great desire to give myself up to your love, to do your will, to consider all that is not you to be nothing. Jesus, you are the only treasure, and now, you even propose to come dwell in my home! Lord, I welcome you.

After he had said this, he went on ahead, going up to Jerusalem (Lk 19:28).

~

Why be frightened [Céline] of not being able to carry the cross without weakening? Jesus fell three times on the road to Calvary and you, poor little child, you will not be like your spouse. You would not want to fall a hundred times if it was necessary to prove your love for him by picking yourself up with more strength than before your fall (LT 81).

~

It is more risky to lead than to follow, and one needs courage to go toward the sacrifice. Jesus, this is the way you climbed the road to Calvary, by falling on the way. I have only to follow, but since the cross is heavy at times, I also fall. By picking myself up, I prove my humble love to you. Lord, give me courage.

Thirty-Third Thursday in Ordinary Time

"[Jerusalem!] If you, even you, had only recognized on this day the things that make for peace!" (Lk 19:42).

~

The more our heart is in heaven, the less we feel the blows….But don't believe this is not a great blessing to feel them, because then our life becomes a martyrdom and Jesus will, one day, reward us. To suffer and be scorned! What bitterness, but what glory! (…) To suffer and more, always….But everything passes (LT 81).

~

Lord Jesus, it is in Jerusalem where you will suffer and be scorned. It will be there where you will give peace forever by the blood of your cross. But it is in the heavenly Jerusalem where your glory will explode. I walk in your tracks in this fleeting world, in the hope you will give me, at the end, in your kingdom of light and peace, the reward of the victorious. Lord, let my heart always be in heaven.

The people were spellbound by what they heard (Lk 19:48).

~

Jesus blessed your child by letting her understand the mysterious depths of charity. If she could express what she understands, you would hear a melody from heaven, but alas! I can only let you hear the stuttering of a child....If the words of Jesus could not help me, I would be tempted to ask your forgiveness and stop writing.... But no, I must continue in obedience what I began in obedience (Ms C, 18v).

~

Lord Jesus, spellbound, tasting what your words make me see, I discover the mysterious charity of the heart of the Holy Trinity. It is a reality that my language could not express, but on which my life depends: all this, thanks to you, Word made incarnate, in the freedom of love. Lord, let your words imprint on my soul.

"Now he is God not of the dead, but of the living; for to him all of them are alive" (Lk 20:38).

~

The saints are not saints because we recognize them as such, and they aren't greater because we write about their life. (...) We will see so many things later! I think sometimes that perhaps I am the fruit of the desires of a little soul to whom I will owe all that I have. So, glory is for God alone; we should not want but one thing: that it come and that we be as happy if it comes through others as through us (CSG 163).

~

Living God, Lord of glory, I get my very existence from you, I live for you. What I am, I owe to your benevolence and to the prayers of my brothers and sisters. What I live, I accomplish for your glory, in the communion of saints. With all of the redeemed, I praise you.

"Jesus, remember me when you come into your kingdom."... "Today, you will be with me in Paradise" (Lk 23:42–43).

～

If I leave the battleground, it isn't with a selfish desire to rest; the thought of the eternal beatitude hardly makes my heart flutter. For a long time, suffering has become my heaven here on earth. (...) What draws me to the heavenly homeland is the Father's call. It is the hope of finally loving him as I so wanted and the thought that I could make him loved by a multitude of souls who would bless him eternally (LT 254).

～

The road of life is difficult. What helps me along my road is knowing you love me and that I was called by you to live forever in the intensity of your love. This is what makes me stay on the battlefield now and until I enter into your kingdom. There, I will intercede so that your love will be known and sought.

"But [the widow] out of her poverty has put in all she had to live on" (Lk 21:4).

～

Oh, what peace floods the soul when it lifts itself beyond human feelings!…No, there is no joy comparable to the joy which those truly poor in spirit feel. If the person, poor in spirit, asks with detachment for something that is necessary; and not only is this refused to him, but an attempt is made to take what he already has, this person must follow Jesus' advice: Give up your coat to he who would like to sue you for your cloak (Ms C, 16v).

～

Even when we are poor and alone, we are attached to what little we do have. What poverty of heart must dwell within us to detach ourselves from our needs, to give up our own sense of self, to let ourselves be prompted to the gift of our poverty, of our destitution. By responding this way, we will feel inner peace. Lord, make me ready to give what is asked of me.

Thirty-Fourth Tuesday in Ordinary Time

"Beware that you are not led astray; for many will come in my name and say, 'I am he!' and 'The time is near!' Do not go after them" (Lk 21:8).

~

Yes, life costs; it is difficult to start a day of hard work. (...) If only we could feel Jesus, oh, we would do anything for him but no, he appears to be a thousand miles away. (...) But what is that gentle friend doing? Doesn't he see the heavy burden that weighs us down? Where is he? Why doesn't he come to comfort us as he is our only friend? (...) He is there, very near. (...) He who begs for this sadness (...) needs it for the souls (LT 57).

~

Jesus, your silence along my route could force me to seek solace elsewhere. How can I carry the heavy burdens and hardships of life alone? You tell me I am going the wrong way. You are the hidden God, living in me, begging for my sorrows to change them into blessings of salvation. Lord, revive your presence in me.

"You will be betrayed even by parents and brothers, by relatives and friends....You will be hated by all because of my name" (Lk 21:16–17).

~

Céline, if you only knew my misery! Oh, if you only knew...holiness doesn't consist of saying nice things, it does not consist of thinking them, or even feeling them!...It consists of suffering, and suffering for it all. (...) Take advantage of our only moment of suffering!... Let us see each moment!...A moment is a treasure. One single act of love will make us know Jesus better....It will bring us closer to him for all eternity (LT 89).

~

Lord, in a fragmented world, almost without evangelic indicators, I suffer at the hands of my loved ones or neighbors because of my faith in you. They do not know you, the founder of my life. May your grace transform my suffering into acts of love and into a way to holiness. May it enlighten those who do not really know you.

"For the powers of the heavens will be shaken. Then they will see 'the Son of Man coming in a cloud' with power and great glory" (Lk 21:26–27).

~

I said that my certainty of going far away from this land of sadness and gloom one day had been given to me as early on as my childhood; (…) I felt the desire for a more beautiful place from the bottom of my heart. (…) I felt that, one day, another place will provide me a stable home. But, all of a sudden, the fog which surrounds me becomes even thicker; it penetrates my soul and surrounds it in such a way that I can't find the gentle image of my homeland there anymore, and everything disappears (Ms C, 6v).

~

If there are times where new heavens and the new land brighten the belief in the Lord's day, times of thick fog could happen and plunge us into darkness. Lord, keep the hope always alive in me of your coming at the end of time. Keep me firm in the assurance of being invited to dwell with you for all time.

Thirty-Fourth Friday in Ordinary Time

"Heaven and earth will pass away, but my words will not pass away" (Lk 21:33).

~

What happiness to be humiliated; it is the only way to become a saint!...Could we now doubt Jesus' will for our souls?...Life is only a dream, and soon we will awaken; what joy....The greater our suffering, the more infinite our glory will be....Oh, let us not fail the trial Jesus sends us; it is a gold mine to take advantage of. Are we going to miss this opportunity? (LT 82).

~

Jesus, you didn't look for humiliation or suffering, but you accepted them in love and they emerged in infinite glory. When I pass from this life, what will be left is an experience of trials that was applied to charity and all the humiliations suffered in love, as a path to holiness suddenly finishing in the vision of glory. Lord, may your full glory finally be revealed to me.

"Be alert at all times, praying that you may have the strength to escape all these things that will take place and to stand before the Son of Man" (Lk 21:36).

~

My path is all trust and all love. I don't understand the souls who are afraid of such a tender friend. Sometimes when I read certain spiritual books, (...) my poor little mind tires very quickly. I close the learned book which strains my mind and dries up my heart, and I take the Holy Bible. Then, all seems bright, (...) I see that it is enough to recognize one's nothingness and to give oneself up like a child, to the arms of God (LT 226).

~

Even with its bumps and obstacles, the path which leads to you, Lord, is one of trust and love. All along the way, each day, your Word keeps my disciple's heart awake. Father, your child gives himself up to you on the day of your Son. Lord, may I be found worthy to stand in your kingdom, in the freedom of love.

Feast Days and Solemn Holy Days of Obligation

The Holy Trinity

"Go therefore and make disciples of all nations, baptizing them in the name of the Father and of the Son and of the Holy Spirit" (Mt 28:19).

~

What a good feeling it brings to think that (...) the whole Trinity is looking at us, is in us, and is pleased to think about us. But what does the Trinity want to see in our hearts? If not "the sound of revelers in a war camp," then "how could we sing the Lord's song in a foreign land?"(...) Our God, the guest in our soul, knows, and so he comes into us, looking to find a home, an empty tent in the middle of the earth's battlegrounds. He asks for no more, and he, the divine musician, takes care of the concert (LT 165).

~

Holy Trinity, guest of my soul since my baptism, make me into a home that is worthy of your presence. Amid the wars on earth, may I know how to adore you, praise you, and sing of you in the festive concert of the angels and saints.

Corpus Christi

"Those who eat my flesh and drink my blood abide in me, and I in them" (Jn 6:56).

~

My heaven is hidden in that small host where Jesus, my Spouse, hides out of love. In that divine home I find life,

and there, my tender savior listens to me, night and day.
What a happy moment it is when, in your tenderness, you
come, my Beloved, and transform me into you. This union
of love, this unfathomable ecstacy, is my heaven! (PN 32).

~

Hidden Lord, through your Eucharist you give me your
Resurrection to transform me into you. I accept you in the
silence of my soul, and our exchange becomes one of love.

The Sacred Heart of Jesus

One of the soldiers pierced his side with a spear, and at
once blood and water came out (Jn 19:34).

~

Ever since it has been given to me to understand the love
in the heart of Jesus, I must admit that he has chased all
the fear from my heart. The memory of my sins shames
me and pushes me to never rely on my strength, which is
only weakness. But, still more, this memory tells me
about mercy and love. When we throw our sins into the
devouring fire of love with a child's trust, how could they
not be irreversibly consumed? (LT 247).

~

Jesus' pierced side is a wound of mercy and love in a sacrificed body. Its forgiveness surges upon me and opens my
life to trust. Lord, let the strength of your love support me.

When the time came for their purification according to the law of Moses, they brought him up to Jerusalem to present him to the Lord...and they offered a sacrifice according to what is stated in the law of the Lord (Lk 2:22–24).

～

Jesus, your arms are the elevator which will lift me to heaven! To achieve this, I must not grow; just the opposite, I must remain small. I must become smaller and smaller. Oh Lord, you have gone beyond my expectations, and I want to sing of your mercies (Ms C, 3r).

～

The child was going to pass from one set of arms to another to become an offering. When your arms will be extended on the cross for the evening sacrifice, Lord Jesus, include me in your offering and lift me up to your Father.

March 19: Saint Joseph

"Joseph, son of David, do not be afraid to take Mary as your wife, for the child conceived in her is from the Holy Spirit. She will bear a son, and you are to name him Jesus" (Mt 1:20–21).

~

Joseph, your admirable life
Was passed in poverty and humility.
But, you were able to contemplate
The beauty of Jesus and Mary.
You were able to contemplate
The beauty of the Son of God,
In his childhood who,
More than once, and gladly,
Submitted in obedience to you
And rested upon your heart (PN 14).

~

Humility as well as beauty are based upon truth. To be true and to welcome the Spirit of truth is the pathway to the future. Holy Joseph, humble and true, lead us on that path.

March 25: The Annunciation of the Lord

"Greetings, favored one! The Lord is with you."…The angel said to her, "Do not be afraid, Mary, for you have found favor with God. And now, you will conceive in your womb and bear a son, and you will name him Jesus" (Lk 1:28,31).

～

When an angel offers you to be the Mother of the God who will reign for all eternity, what an astonishing mystery to see you prefer the unutterable treasure of your virginity! I understand that your soul, oh Immaculate Virgin, would be more dear to the Lord than the Divine sojourn. I understand that your soul, humble and gentle valley, would contain my Jesus, the Ocean of Love (PN 54).

～

By conceiving Jesus, the Ocean of Love, your virginal being becomes the jewel box for the precious pearl, offered by the Father to all humanity. You are blessed, Mary, Mother of God.

May 31: The Visitation of Mary

"Blessed are you among women, and blessed is the fruit of your womb. And why has this happened to me, that the mother of my Lord comes to me? (…) And blessed is she who believed" (Lk 1:42–43, 45).

～

To ask something of the Blessed Virgin Mary is not the same as asking God. She knows what she has to do about my small desires, if she must say them or not…. Finally, it is for her to see, not to force God to fulfill me, to leave him free to do his will (CSG 49).

~

Mary, Mother of Jesus, stay close to me. You are the mother in whom I confide. Of my profuse requests, present only those to the Lord that correspond to his will.

June 24: The Birth of Saint John the Baptist

Then they began motioning to his father to find out what name he wanted to give him. He asked for a writing tablet and wrote, "His name is John" (Lk 1:62–63).

~

I asked myself what name I would have at Carmel. I knew that there already was a Sister Thérèse of Jesus there; yet, my pretty name "Thérèse" could not be taken away from me. All at once, I thought of the little Jesus who I loved so much and I said to myself: "Oh, how happy I would be to call myself Thérèse of the Child Jesus" (Ms A, 31r–v).

~

A name labels a person or reveals their mission, like John the Baptist or Thérèse with her little way. May my patron saint be my model, may I live the meaning of my name.

June 29: Saints Peter and Paul, Apostles

"Simon son of John, do you love me?"…"Lord, you know everything; you know that I love you."…"Feed my sheep" (Jn 21:17).

~

How did Jesus love his disciples and why did he love them? It wasn't their human qualities that attracted him; an infinite distance existed between them. He was knowledge, Eternal Wisdom; they were poor sinners—ignorant, filled with worldly thoughts. Yet, Jesus calls them his friends, his brothers. He wants to open his Father's kingdom for them and see them reign with him in this kingdom. He wants to die on a cross because he said: "There is no greater love than to give one's life for those we love" (Ms C, 12r).

~

How could I tell you of my love if you hadn't first demonstrated yours to me by your call for me and by the supreme gift of your life? My love for you is but a humble copy of your love for me. Lord, I love you, today and forever.

July 16: Our Lady of Mount Carmel

All who heard it were amazed at what the shepherds told them. But Mary treasured all these words and pondered them in her heart (Lk 2:18–19).

~

Close to you, Oh my loving Mother, I have found rest for my heart; I want nothing more on earth. Jesus alone is my entire happiness. If, at times, I feel sadness, if fear assails me, always, by supporting my weakness, Mother, you have deemed to bless me (PN 7).

Virgin Mother, Jesus was your total joy. You looked upon him with the eyes of your heart. When the road is rough, and the sorrow is heavy, may your motherly heart help me see the true meaning of events.

August 6: Transfiguration of the Lord

He was transfigured before them, and his face shone like the sun, and his clothes became dazzling white (Mt 17:2).

Your Face is my only wealth, I ask for nothing more. By continuously hiding myself in it, I will look like you, Jesus. Leave in me the Divine imprint of your Features, filled with kindness. And soon, I will become a saint, and to you, I will draw hearts (PN 20).

May your radiant face leave its imprint in me. May your transfigured being fascinate my eyes. Lord of Glory, may I become what you want me to be; a saint by grace.

August 15: The Assumption of the Blessed Virgin Mary

"My spirit rejoices in God my Savior, for he has looked with favor on the lowliness of his servant. Surely, from now on all generations will call me blessed" (Lk 1:47–48).

◡

The Blessed Virgin was also watching over her little flower. Not wanting her to be tarnished by contact with earthly things, she moved her to her mountain before she bloomed....While waiting for this happy moment, the little Thérèse grew in love for the Heavenly Mother (Ms A, 40r).

◡

I glorify you, Lord, because of the Blessed Virgin Mary, who watches over me. I feel joyful in you because of the one who looks after me with a true heart. While she lives forever in your glory, draw me in to your home with prayer.

September 8: Birth of the Blessed Virgin Mary

Look, the virgin shall conceive and bear a son, and they shall name him Emmanuel, which means, "God is with us" (Mt 1:23).

◡

*On the morning of September 8 (1890), I felt flooded
with a river of peace and it was in this peace "surpassing
all feelings" that I pronounced my Holy Vows….My
union with Jesus happened, not in the midst of thunder
and lightning, that is to say extraordinary blessings, but
in the midst of a gentle breeze. (…) I offered myself to
Jesus so he could carry out his will in me perfectly,
without any humans ever putting any obstacles there (Ms
A, 76v).*

~

Blessed Virgin Mary, as you offered yourself to the action
of the Holy Spirit in you, as you welcomed the Word made
flesh into your womb, in this way I offer myself to your
Son, Emmanuel. May I faithfully fulfill the will of the Father.

September 14: The Holy Cross

"So must the Son of Man be lifted up, that whoever believes in him may have eternal life" (Jn 3:14–15).

~

*Let us not believe that it is possible to love without
suffering, without suffering a great deal….That is our
poor human nature and it is not there for nothing!…It is
our wealth, our livelihood! It is so precious that Jesus
came on earth just to have it (LT 89).*

~

To love and be loved brings about suffering, since it is, at the same time, opening oneself to another all the way to the ultimate gift of forgiveness and allowing oneself to be opened all the way to the possible failure of misunderstanding. Jesus' path of love becomes my own.

October 1: Saint Thérèse of the Child Jesus

"I thank you, Father, Lord of heaven and earth, because you have hidden these things from the wise and the intelligent and have revealed them to infants" (Mt 11:25).

~

I could only do a very few things, or rather nothing, if I was alone. What comforts me is to think that, at your side, I could be of some use. In fact, the zero, by itself, has no value, but placed next to a number, it becomes powerful, provided that it is put on the right side, after, not before it! That is where Jesus has put me (LT 226).

~

My knowledge cannot bring me to understand your mystery. But placed next to Jesus' heart, I share his wisdom, I receive his brotherly knowledge and his love. I stay a little one, who praises and loves you, God of love.

October 15: Saint Thérèse of Jesus (Ávila)

"Let anyone who is thirsty come to me, and let the one who believes in me drink. As the scripture has said, 'Out of the believer's heart shall flow rivers of living water'" (Jn 7:37–38).

〜

I need a heart burning with tenderness
To remain my means of support forever,
To love everything in me, even my weakness…
Not to leave me, night and day.
I couldn't find anyone
Who would love me forever, never to die.
I need a God to take my human nature
To become my brother and be able to suffer (PN 23).

〜

From the wound in your heart, where life and love spring forth, from your glorified holy humanity, in which I find support and tenderness, I receive the life-giving water that satisfies my thirst to love you. It helps me go beyond my weakness and bonds me with you forever.

November 1: All Saints' Day

"Blessed are the poor in spirit, for theirs is the kingdom of heaven" (Mt 5:3).

~

Once, I wondered why God does not give equal glory to the chosen ones in heaven. I was afraid that they would not all be happy; then Pauline told me to go get Papa's big glass and put it next to my small thimble and fill them both up with water. Then, she asked me which one was fuller. I told her that they were both equally full, and it was impossible to add any more water than they could hold. (…) In heaven, God would give as much glory to the chosen ones as they could handle; and this way, the last would have no reason to envy the first (Ms A, 19v).

~

We would be happy in heaven if our poverty allows God to fill us with his life of love and makes us shine in his reflected glory. Shining city around the Lamb, lit radiantly by the variety of saints, each one is happy with their share of blessings.

November 2: All Souls' Day

"Jesus, remember me when you come into your king-dom."…Truly I tell you, today you will be with me in Para-dise" (Lk 23:42–43).

~

I feel it, we must go to heaven by the same route, the one of suffering united with love. When I reach the harbor, I will teach you (…) how to navigate on the stormy sea of the world, with the abandon and love of a child who knows that his Father cherishes him and would not leave him alone in a time of danger (LT 258).

~

This bandit attached to the cross had navigated the paths of the world. His suffering differed from yours, Jesus. But he heard: "Father forgive them." He who gives himself to you, confident of your love, will see his path transfigured.

November 9: Dedication of Saint John Lateran

Use readings on page 297.

December 8: The Immaculate Conception of the Blessed Virgin Mary

The virgin's name was Mary...."Greetings, favored one! The Lord is with you" (Lk 1:27–28).

～

Finding no assistance on earth, poor little Thérèse turned to her heavenly mother. She prayed to her to have pity on her. ...All of a sudden, the Blessed Virgin Mary appeared beautiful to me, with a beauty such as I had never seen before. Her face radiated an indescribable kindness and tenderness. But what penetrated my soul to its very depth was the "ravishing smile of the Blessed Virgin" (Ms A, 30r).

～

You are so beautiful, Mary, full of grace. Your femininity explains your gentleness of heart. Your glance is filled with charity. Smile of God in our world, intercede for us.

December 14: Saint John of the Cross

"Righteous Father, the world does not know you, but I know you....I made your name known to them, and I will make it known, so that the love with which you have loved me may be in them, and I in them" (Jn 17:25–26).

⁓

Jesus, I am too small to do big things...and my fantasy is to hope that your love accepts me as a victim....My fantasy is to beg the eagles, my brothers, to grant me the favor of flying toward the Sun of love with the very wings of the Divine Eagle (Ms B, 5v).

⁓

How will I get all the way to you if you don't come to get me to lift me up to the divine horizons? Like the eagle facing the sun, draw me to you by your bright power of love. By loving you, I will be able to offer myself to you.

By the Same Author

Les Liturgies de l'Assemblée (Liturgies of the Congregation), Droguet-Ardant, Fleurus-Mame, Paris, 1969.

Ton Dieu marche avec toi (Your God Walks with You), CLD, Chambray-lès-Tours, 1972.

Sur la route pascale de Jésus, avec St. Thérèse d'Avila (On the Paschal Road of Jesus, with St. Teresa of Avila), in collaboration with the Carmelites of Laval, Téqui, Paris, 1986.

La Cinquantaine pascale avec les Saints du Carmel (The Fifty Days of Easter with the Carmelite Saints), in collaboration with the Carmelites of Laval, Téqui, Paris, 1986.

Te suivre, Jésus, Sauveur de l'homme (Following You, Jesus, Savior of Mankind), guided by Saint John of the Cross, in collaboration with the Carmelites of Laval, Téqui, Paris, 1988.

Prier 15 jours avec Jean de la Croix (15 Days of Prayers with Saint John of the Cross), Nouvelle Cité, Paris, 1990; third edition, 1996.

L'Année du Seigneur avec les Saints du Carmel (The Year of Our Lord with the Carmelite Saints), Téqui, Paris, 1995.

Prier 15 jours avec Thérèse de Lisieux (15 Days of Prayers with Saint Thérèse of Lisieux), Nouvelle Cité, Paris, 1996.